LIFE IS
WHAT YOU
MAKE IT

Other Newt List books by Ernest Holmes

Creative Mind

Creative Mind and Success

Ernest Holmes Speaks

How to Use Your Power:
20 Practical Lessons for Creating A Balanced Life

60 Meditations for a Mindful Life

The Basics of Spiritual Mind Healing

The Bible in Light of Spiritual Philosophy

The Meaning of the Bible

The Philosophy of Emerson

The Philosophy of Jesus

LIFE IS
WHAT YOU
MAKE IT

Ernest Holmes

with Frederick Bailes

**newt
LIST**

Newt List

Chicago • New York

Copyright © 2015 by Randall Friesen
Updated and gender-neutral

Newt List
www.NewtList.com

ISBN 978-0-69-2450246

Printed in the United States of America
Published October 2015

Design by Randall Friesen

CONTENTS

FOREWORD

⁓

At the heart of the Science of Mind philosophy is a practical and direct approach to spirituality. It invites the student to meet life not with fear, but with excitement and a sense of adventure; with the attitude that anyone who understands the ideas of Science of Mind can apply them for beneficial changes in their life. The ideas are both ancient and modern: the outer experience of life reflects the inner state of mind; inner states of mind can be changed; and regular spiritual practice reveals the essential benevolent nature of life. Ernest Holmes summarizes these and additional spiritual ideas with remarkable clarity in *Life Is What You Make It*.

Prayer treatment is the practical application of these life changing ideas taught by Science of Mind. It is a form of affirmative prayer that is substantially different from conventional prayer in that it is not a petition to a distant deity, but rather more like directed meditation on a specific topic, and with a specific outcome in mind.

Ernest Holmes writes that the heart of prayer treatment is that moment when, in your prayer, you come into a quiet realization of the truth of what you are saying. To me, the central values of Science of Mind are: that through practice we become reacquainted with the nature of reality: that life responds to us: and that the more clearly we approach it in our minds, the more powerful its response. The practice then is to become clear on our approach to life, clearing away doubt, fear, inherited thought tendencies and all other concepts that act like barriers between us and the magnificence of God "in which we move and have our being."

Edward Viljoen, D.D.
Senior Minister, Center for Spiritual Living
Santa Rosa, California

LIFE IS
WHAT YOU
MAKE IT

The Fundamental Principle

In this introductory chapter, we must establish a fundamental truth, which is "Life is what you make it." This may sound trite, but it is basic to a book such as this because in seeing truth, we must establish ourselves on a foundation of intellectual honesty. If we shrink from facing facts, we flee to unreality and build on an unsound foundation. As a result, the whole superstructure that we erect will be unsound.

The Fundamental Principle

Life is too serious to be taken in anything less than a face-to-face way. Life always seems harsh and severe to those who refuse to face it squarely. Since our purpose is to make life our servant instead of our master, our fundamental premise must be established in the cold, naked truth. This premise is that our outer *seen* life is an exact duplication of our inner *unseen* thought life.

Others may deny this principle, argue with it or ignore it, but it does not alter the fact. This principle operates relentlessly whether we agree or disagree with it, and the wise person is the one who, understanding a principle, begins to cooperate with it. Unwise people evade or run counter to it and are hurt by it, or rather are hurt by their own foolish non-cooperation with that principle.

The Outer Like the Inner

How do we know that our fundamental premise is true? This is a fair question and one that warrants our taking time enough for investigation.

Some time ago, a business owner came in for a consultation. His business was falling off. He said that he had increased his advertising budget recently because he had always found advertising to be productive of sales. He had also put on additional sales staff. Yet in spite of his increased effort, his volume of business had steadily declined. He said that he could not understand this, because these increased efforts seemed to indicate that his thought was on better business.

As we talked, it developed that several business houses dealing in a similar line had failed recently, and buried far beneath the surface of his thought was the fear that he, too, might succumb to the prevailing business depression. Further, he suspected that his sales staff was "laying down on the job," as he put it. In other words, fear and suspicion were the dominant notes in his life. His outer gestures indicated confidence; his inner, almost hidden thoughts were of an opposite nature. This was pointed out to him and instruction given as to what he must do to change his inner attitudes into ones of confidence and expectancy of the good instead of the bad. He changed his general way of thinking. Gradually, as his inner confidence grew, his thought reflected this change, until the growth was phenomenal. But the growth did not come until the negative fear thought was deliberately replaced by a new line of confident expectation.

The outer change never fails to come when the inner thought is intelligently changed. The reason for this fact is that we are all Mind. We are not physical organisms containing and using minds; we are each Mind using a body. This Mind built the body as a vehicle for intelligence and expresses its thoughts in physical form, appearance and circumstances. Thus, all the exterior happenings in our lives are merely extensions of our own thoughts.

Bodily Attitudes Reflect the Inner Life

We have said that our appearance or facial expression is the effect of our thought. This can be observed very readily. We say of certain people, "They have a kind face, or a hard face," etc. By this we mean that their thoughts have evidently been of a kindly nature—or the reverse—for so long that the inner thought has drawn the face into lines that correspond to itself. The eye gradually takes on the reflection of the inner thought life.

We see some people and we say, "What sour expressions those people have!" Life has whipped them so often or for so long that their inner consciousness of defeat has written itself in their expressions, in the furtive look of their eyes, perhaps in the very stoop of their shoulders. And this is all entirely unconscious. If someone acquaints these people with the fact that they have a certain expression, they may endeavor to throw it off through conscious effort. But if their hidden thought life is still one of defeat or cruelty or avarice, as the case may be, the change that they try to assume will be very short-lived unless the inner thought is entirely changed.

Just one more illustration concerning outer form and its correspondence to inward thought. The petulant individual or the angry one assumes a pouting expression or draws the mouth into a hard line when upset. Along with this, creases appear between the eyes. After one has done this many times, the hard mouth-line and the creases become deepened and assume more or less of a permanent character. Thus we can judge the quality of a person's habitual thinking. In other words, Mind writes the story of its activity clearly on the pages of the face.

Changing These Attitudes

If we wish to change these outer expressions, we must change our thinking, because outward changes can come only when the inner thought life is changed. If we could take selfish people and replace their thoughts with those of a sincere interest in others, as frequently has happened when one has had a real change of heart, then without any conscious effort at changing the exterior, the facial expression will automatically change in line with the inward change. If defeated people can be brought into an inner consciousness of victory, there soon appears new life to their steps, new forthrightness in their aspects, and the appearance of adequacy to meet any situation. In other words, those people come to bear expressions of being "sure of themselves."

Inner Thought and Health

Just as it is true that the outer appearance corresponds to the inner quality of thought, so it is also true in regard to other physical conditions. In other words, one's health is the direct result of one's habitual inward mental state.

We have all seen how the inward mental state of anger has a direct effect on the body. It causes the face to flush and the fingers involuntarily to clench. A sudden great fear will send the blood away from the face causing it to turn pale. This explains why people who have lived under long continued worry or fear are inclined to develop the physical disorder called anemia. Just as the often-repeated petulant attitude will gradually give a habitually petulant expression—a crossness often indulged in will produce the deep "bad-tempered" creases—so the long continued fear thought eventually has its physical counterpart in some form of physical disease, such as anemia.

Angry Thoughts

Most people have noticed that an angry discussion just before eating or at the dinner table takes the appetite away. It causes changes in the secretions of the stomach, which make it unwise to attempt to eat, because the stomach is not in fit condition to carry on the process of digestion when in this condition. Fear, anger, etc. can in this way lead gradually to a condition of ulcer of the stomach. Again, let us remember that this is all unconscious as an effect. It is true, nevertheless, as we stated at the beginning, that "Life is what you make it." The inner thought life controls the outer material experience because we are Mind using the body as a vehicle for our thoughts.

A Highway to Happiness

In later chapters, we will study the true scientific method of changing the thought life clear down to its depths and will uncover laws of thought that bring you into the true realization of your own inherent inner powers, bringing your own thinking under the influence of tried and tested principles of constructive thought so that you can enjoy a complete mental house-cleaning. This does not call for advanced education or great willpower; it calls for careful attention to deep underlying principles, principles which, when grasped, will change the entire thought life and put you in touch with your highest self.

We were not sent into the world to live a defeated, sick, unhappy life. We are ordained to happiness, health and prosperity. The whole scheme of the universe is that of a benevolent conspiracy to grant us the very best. But we must get ourselves straight on this one thing, which is that *no one can rob us of happiness or can achieve happiness for us but ourselves.* If we will grant this fundamental premise, we can go on to make of life whatever we desire. If we try to evade this truth, our life will be spent in the shallows close to the shore, where self-pity, whining and complaining about "circumstances" will be our unhappy lot.

Inner Thought and Finance

This same truth operates in our financial affairs just as it does in our appearance and our health. Those who are defeated financially are in this condition because deep down in their hidden thought lives they do not really believe they can have money. There is much more to this statement than appears on the surface, so you would be wise not to reject it at this stage. As you progress in your study, you will see that there is only one law in the universe and that this law applies in exactly the same manner in your health, appearance, happiness, prosperity, indeed in everything that you desire.

In a later chapter, we will go into the procedure to be followed to create what we might call the money-consciousness, but it is sufficient at this stage to say that the very moment you stop hindering money from manifesting in your affairs, it will begin to flow toward you. When we remember that we are Mind and that money has no preferences, being entirely a neutral thing, then we begin to understand why money flows in the direction to which it is attracted and flows away from the point where it is being repelled.

The money-less person is actually repelling money. Again, let us repeat that this repulsion of money is entirely an unconscious thing, just as is the repulsion of health. The old statement "Those that have get" is true not because somewhere in a far-off heaven there sits a person called God who gives freely to one and withholds from another, but because those who have achieved money have done so due to the fact that their inner thought life attracted money, and this attractive quality that drew it to them in the first place continues to bring more. In other words, they are alive to money. This is why when some cataclysm has stripped these types of people from their fortunes, they have gone out again and run a shoestring into another fortune.

Law, Not Chance, Governs

There are laws by which all this occurs, even the loss of money on the part of one who has made it. But the fact remains that the ups and downs of life follow clearly defined principles of thought, and that those who understand and practice the principles of success will gain success. It is just as impossible for a person to have success following the methods of failure as it would be to experience failure when following the methods of success. So you may take courage at this point and rest in the quiet inner assurance that you can have those things you desire when you go after them in the right way. As the lessons arrive and are mastered, you will find that a fundamental change has occurred in your thinking, a change that is constantly proving itself in your increasing health, prosperity and happiness.

∽

Meditation

Today I make a new venture in the realm of thought. I am determined to use my mind consciously and constructively to improve my health and my condition. I resolve to banish every thought of anxiety and fear. I will believe that there is a power in the universe that is available and trustworthy. I will entertain no angry or envious thoughts. I will dwell only on what is true, what is worthy, what is right, what is pure, what is amiable, what is kindly, on everything that is excellent or praiseworthy. I believe that these attitudes of mind, persisted in, will bring to me greater peace, happiness and health. I believe that, with an inflow of peace and health, my conditions will be improved. I am ready to prove this to myself, and I resolve to persist until my outer experiences are a duplication of my thought.

∽

Questions

1. What is the fundamental principle of the Science of Mind philosophy?
2. What type of thought may bring business troubles?
3. Does thought affect health?
4. Are we ever governed by chance?
5. How can we achieve happiness?

Answers

1. The fundamental principle of the Science of Mind philosophy is that our outer life is an exact duplication of our inner thought life.
2. If fear of failure and competition or suspicion of one's co-workers dominate our thought, these thoughts will eventually express in disturbed and unsatisfactory business conditions.
3. Anger has a physical reaction and often affects the digestion. Fear also acts like anger, to which it is related. While most of the effects are due to unconscious thought or combinations of thought, always they are determining factors in bodily conditions.
4. All of life is governed by law, never by chance. We bring to ourselves good or evil, prosperity or adversity in accordance with our use of impersonal mental law.
5. Happiness is a thing of thought with the individual. No one can take it from us but ourselves. No one can give it to us but ourselves. We must control our thought life in order to achieve it.

How We Think

❧

At the outset, we should go briefly into the mechanics of the thought life. Many people already know and understand these, but since this book is designed to take you from the place where you are now to the place you would like to be, we will outline certain terms so that when they are mentioned later they will be clearly understood by everyone.

Levels of Living

We live on three levels: spiritual, mental and physical. Spirit reasons, chooses and decides what it wants; Mind carries out these decisions; and the outer physical is the result. By the physical we mean not only the body but all of our material affairs, including our home, business and finances. We need not take time to go into any detailed explanation of the physical, but it is important for you to clearly understand exactly how your mind works, because your whole success hinges on a proper understanding of this.

Conscious and Subconscious Mind

From the beginning of the history of humankind, we have been thinkers and have been intensely interested in our own thinking ability. Up until recent years, the world's philosophers had classed all our mental activities into one group. Whatever we think, they said, we think with our "mind." But in the nineteenth century, certain psychologists began to make a distinction between those thought processes of which we were conscious and those of which we were not conscious.

They observed, for example, that in picking up a stone and throwing it at a target, we used conscious, choosing mental activity, but that in walking, we did not consciously move one foot after the other; we simply walked without consciously thinking of the method of walking. We could be using our conscious thought activity in reading while unconsciously moving our legs in walking. During the daytime, we would be thinking consciously of our various activities, but we noticed that when we went to sleep, we were not thinking consciously. Nevertheless, in our dreams we were having experiences, perhaps traveling to a far country or being chased by a maniac. The experience was a thought process, yet it was not consciously selected and carried out.

This led close observers to make a distinction between what they called "conscious" mind (the conscious) and "subconscious" mind (the conscious and subconscious phases of the one mind). These terms are now giving way to the words *objective* for conscious, and *subjective* for the subconscious.

Objective Mind

Objective mind is the phase of mind that reasons, chooses, observes, judges, estimates and decides. Its chief characteristic is that it has the power of choice. Soldiers may be terrified at the idea of going into battle. If they force themselves to go, it is done through the activity of their objective mind, which tells them that soldiers have to go into battle. This process might follow the line of reasoning that it is their duty as good soldiers to go, or it might follow the reasoning that they will be shot at sunrise for refusing orders. Either way, it is a process of reasoning and choice. When we want to scratch our nose, we have to choose to lift our arm from our side to do it. This may be an instantaneous process of choice, but it is the product of a reasoning process.

Subjective Mind

Subjective mind, on the other hand, never reasons. Its chief characteristic is to obey the choice of the objective mind. It is always the servant of objective mind, yet its power and scope are far greater than that of objective mind. It is estimated that ninety percent of our mental activities are subjective. It is as though an elephant was following the directions of an ant. All the elephant's tremendous strength would be entirely at its service to lift and move heavy things that the tiny strength of the ant could not budge.

When we come to the matter of healing disease or developing courage and self-confidence, or producing conditions that seem far beyond our ability to create, we will see the significance of a clear understanding of this relationship between objective and subjective mind, and of this characteristic of the subjective obedience.

Subjective mind is a highly intelligent mind, but it is not a reasoning mind. Its intelligence is perfect. It knows how to do anything. It has all knowledge. It knows how to create anything that ever was created. It knows how to build a body because it built every body that ever was built. It knows how to build new, healthy cells in place of sickly ones.

Subjective mind knows how to make supply flow in the direction to which it is ordered. It knows how to increase business and to attract customers and friends. It knows how every successful business is run and how every successful life is achieved. It keeps the heart beating in the body. It keeps the cells absorbing nutrients. It keeps the nerves in condition to transmit lightning messages from one part of the body to another. In fact, subjective mind is the worker that has created every objective thing in the entire universe.

Microcosm and Macrocosm

In order to better understand this, it might be well to go back to the creation of the universe, because humankind is on a small scale what God is on a large scale. The same creative process by which a world is constructed is used in building a new set of circumstances for us. By coming to a real understanding of this fact, we can remake our little world.

Just as there is a trinity in us of Spirit, Mind and Body, so there is a cosmic trinity. "In the beginning, God created the heavens and the earth." God is Spirit; Mind is the power that knows itself; Spirit has the power to carry out every desire. When God speaks, Mind moves into action to produce that which it is the will of Spirit to create. This act of creation is not the making of something out of nothing, but the bringing of the substance of Spirit into form. It is some act of Spirit within and upon itself. Creation is the bringing into form of this previously formless substance. In other words, God spoke the word, and Mind carried it out unquestioningly and brought the universe into substantial form. Thus the universe that we see is in reality a spiritual system composed of spiritual substance and is as truly an expression of God as are Spirit and Mind.

Only One Mind

There is only one Mind in the universe. The same Mind that formed the granite mountain formed the grass of the field and the human body. We will come to see that the human body, created out of this formless substance, is likewise spiritual substance, and its form and condition of health follows the activity of Mind under the direction of Spirit. In the meantime, we will content ourselves with knowing that this obedient, responsive Mind, which has all knowledge and can create anything, is as a great, unseen ocean pervading and filling the entire universe. Leading out of this fact is the second important truth: That which we call our subjective mind is merely the portion or quantity of this great ocean of subjectivity that we are using at any particular time.

We have at our instantaneous disposal the greatest—in fact, the only—power in the universe. It is entirely subject to us and our will, and will work obediently for us in a constructive way when we understand how to direct its activity. The illustration of the giant elephant is totally inadequate to convey the full picture of the unlimited power that we have at our disposal awaiting our word.

Why People Fail

If this is all true and we have at our fingertips such a tremendous flow of power waiting to be directed toward the solution of our problems, the logical question that arises is, "Why does anyone ever fail?" Here is a statement of fact as to the availability of unlimited assistance. Yet on every hand we see people struggling weakly in the grasp of circumstances, pleading with God to lighten their loads, running back and forth seeking some way of escape and giving way to the blankness of despair. What a bleak picture! Human beings, the crown of creation made in the image and likeness of God, scourged by our fears and cringing in a dark corner, afraid of life and sometimes even seeking death at our own hand!

One reason why people fail is that they break away from God's method of creation, and therefore they are unable to create for themselves. They see two or more things, not one. They see and know the thing they want, but they also constantly see another picture of some power, force, circumstance or influence that is bigger than themselves, which they think is able to stop them from getting what they want.

"The double-minded are unstable in all their ways. Let not those think they will receive anything." "If your eye is single, your whole body shall be full of light."

These are two statements of a fundamental truth, which is that any idea held steadily in Mind is bound to reproduce itself in the outer life. It is unthinkable to imagine that Spirit decided what it wanted to create and then began to wonder if some power could hinder it from creating it. God saw what God wanted, God knew that God could create it, and God spoke the word to decree it without the slightest wavering. God said, "Let there be…" and there was.

We fail to hold unswervingly to a single picture, the picture of the thing we want and the fact that it is now ours. Our double-mindedness produces a distortion that can manifest only in distorted circumstances. Just as a person whose eyes focus imperfectly sees two pictures overlapping and dimming one another, so the untrained mind sees two pictures—the thing wanted and the hindering force—both of which manifest to the degree that they are seen.

Fear Is a Squatter

Fear is our chief obstacle to singular vision. Fear is the greatest liar in the universe. Moreover, it is always squatting on territory in which it has no rights. Yet it lies so expertly that most people do not see through it. Most people fail to see that their *mental world* is *more real* than their *material world*, and that through their imagination fear can paint a picture that can cause the same mental distress that would come from an actual experience.

For example, if you were left alone in a lonely mountain cabin and were dominated by fear, you could go through all the torture that would be yours in an actual experience by allowing your imagination to tell you that someone is prowling around outside. Every rustle of a branch on the roof, every falling pine cone can cause your heart to beat wildly, cold perspiration to break out on you and may bring you into a hysterical condition, even to the verge of insanity. And over what? *Over nothing at all,* nothing that has any basis in reality.

There is only one thing to do with fear, and that is to *face it.* Fear will never accept a good look in its face. If you had allowed your objective mind to *choose* and had gone outside to search all around the cabin, you would have found that your suffering was completely caused by your imagination. Fear always seizes on nothing and tries to fool us into believing it is something.

∽

Meditation

There is no fear in love, because perfect love casts out all fear. I now recognize that the ultimate nature of the universe is love. Since the universe is an expression of love and I am some part of the universe, I know that love dwells in me. It is in me in all its fullness, freedom and infinity. This must be so, because God is love, and Spirit is always present in all its fullness at any point, at any time. Since I am a partaker of this divine love-nature, which is free and perfect, there is no room in me for fear. Love lives in me and casts out all fear.

∽

Questions

1. What do we mean by objective mind?
2. What is the chief characteristic of subjective mind?
3. What is the real meaning of creation?
4. What is the subjective mind?
5. How do we use creative power?

Answers

1. By objective mind, we mean the self-conscious mind that reasons inductively and makes choices.
2. The chief characteristic of subjective mind is its complete obedience to objective mind. It reasons deductively only, taking any statement at face value and bringing it to its logical conclusion.
3. Creation is not making something out of nothing, but the bringing of substance into form in correspondence to thought or choice.
4. There is only one Mind. The subjective phase of our mind is our individual use of the universal subjective Mind.
5. Spirit creates by contemplation, and what it contemplates, it becomes. We use this same creative power by holding ideas steadily in mind until they reproduce in form and condition

The Influence of Fear

Let us examine further the influence of fear. Imagine that you want a larger income. You have persuaded yourself that you have equal ability with others who earn such incomes, and you decide that you are going to have it. So far, so good. But then as you begin to feel the warm, anticipatory glow of possession, fear sneaks up behind you and whispers, "Just look around and see how many people there are with better education and more ability than you have. Even they are having a hard time making ends meet. Remember, times are tough. People are being laid off. There are three people for every job now. Besides, you have always been unlucky. Others have always gotten better breaks than you. You don't seem to have the nerve and push that is needed to break into the bigger money."

Your desire for the larger income may be just as great as before the inward discussion, but you have allowed fear to implant several other contradictory pictures in your thought. And since your past experience agrees with these whispers of fear, you allow those experiences a parking space in your mind, and of course they then manifest in your experience. Instead of your mind being single, di-

19

rected to the one point of your desire, it is multiple, scattered, hazy. And hazy thinking will always produce hazy results.

Power of Imagination

Imagination is one of the gifts bestowed on the individual, the thinker, but we have allowed it to become degraded into a curse. We should use it as we were intended to use it: to lift us to the heights. But fear has settled on the land that should be occupied by confidence, and we, its rightful owners, have allowed it to swagger around as if it had rights. *Fear has no rights and would have none at any time unless we allowed it to have them.*

Since imagination has been preempted by fear with the result that we have been kept from our rightful heritage, we can reverse this process. Those of us who go about this seriously can gradually fill the imagination with pictures that support our big desire, so that when we start to apply mental law for our own benefit, our contributory mental states will form a positive, constructive background that will hasten the accomplishment of the good. Those of us who follow these lessons along to their conclusion and begin to apply them as rapidly as we get them will find that, no matter what the experience of our next-door neighbor may be, we can lift ourselves into a position of mastery. We are the children of a sovereign, and we can learn to reign like one.

The Influence of Faith

Having dealt with the effect of fear in the case of seeking to create a larger income, let us look at the effect of faith. You are now going to change your method. Instead of allowing fear pictures to crowd in on your big desire, you are going to bring forth *faith pictures*.

Sit quietly and think over all the reasons why you should be in possession of more money, greater happiness and security, nicer things for you and your family, a sense of achievement, etc. Now, convince yourself of the fact that God is not withholding supply from you; that God will give you as much as you yourself decide to take; that what you get in your outer world is not dependent on the whim of some capricious deity, *but on your own use of mental law.*

You should convince yourself that your paycheck is a reflection of the inner conviction of your worth and your determination to achieve it. You should believe that the great ocean of subjective mind will produce what you want when you go after it with a single mind, and that neither hell nor high water can keep you from getting it. Convince yourself that conditions, depressions, shortage of jobs do not apply to you. They apply only to those who fear them. Know that you have been endowed with the same Mind that has always brought success to the prosperous and that your mind has great creative power because it is the Mind that created the universe and all the wealth that is in it.

Money Is a Spiritual Idea

Money, being a neutral thing, has no preference. It does not like one person more than another. It will flow toward those who, by holding a single mind toward it, attract it, welcome it, expect it, and know that they are its master. The years of lack through which you have gone have been unnecessary. There has always been an unlimited source of supply for you, and although you are unconscious of it, is your fault—and yours alone—that you have failed to tap that source. Mind creates money just as easily as it creates air.

We must correct the belief that money is hard to get. After all, money is no harder for Mind to create than sand. We have placed a higher value on gold than on sand only because gold is scarcer. But Mind could have made the sands of the shores of all the oceans from solid gold just as easily as from rock.

What is money? Money is the medium we use to get food with which to sustain life. A tree or a blade of grass has no possible use for money, but they both need supply just the same. In order to live and grow, they must have nutrients. They get them inherently from the soil by way of moisture. So the nutrients of moisture and money are the very same thing, only in different form. They are both necessary means of maintaining life.

The tree expects nutrients and sends its roots always expectantly for them. We humans, on the contrary, think up all the reasons why we cannot get sufficient supply. And here is where we get in our own way and keep ourselves limited, because we keep Mind, which would just as readily bring us money, constantly on the job of keeping money *away* from us. Remember, subjective mind does not reason. It does not feel sorry for you and say, "You're having a tough time, so I'll draw money to you." It knows only to obey your thought, and your thoughts are, "Times are tough. Money is hard to get," etc., etc.

The Attitude of Expectancy

The tree expects food, the seagull flying around the beach expects food, and the innumerable millions of insects expect food. "Your heavenly Creator feeds them; are you not much better than they?" We are better in that we are thinkers and can definitely set this law into action to keep good away from us. We have looked around on millions of underprivileged and underfed people and have set our expectancy on the idea of limitation. This is a fear picture. *Human beings are the only living creatures that worry and thus draw lack to themselves.* We must change this underlying thought pattern and know within ourselves that we are dealing with a neutral law of Mind that will proceed to draw money toward us in the measure of our expectancy.

It is imperative that you disabuse your mind of the false notion that money or health or any other desirable thing is something that you may or may not get according to the "will of God." God has endowed us with the ability to get what we want and has placed at our disposal the law of Mind by which we ourselves can get it.

The Basis for Expectancy

You will see how marvelously this knowledge will add to your efficiency. Instead of wondering *whether* you can get things, you now know you *can* get them. Instead of wondering whether you are doomed to a life of defeat, you now know you are doomed to nothing but that to which you doom yourself. You are not a plaything of an inscrutable Providence. You are not a chip flung out onto the ocean of life. You can truly say, "I am master of my fate; I am captain of my soul."

We have too long believed ourselves "born to trouble as the sparks fly upward." We must deliberately dislodge this suicidal thought by pouring in the certain knowledge that we are destined to the biggest, fullest, richest expression of life and happiness. We must know that the whole purpose of creation is one thing: to express God. Spirit evidently needed concrete forms through which to express. The body of God, that great, unformed substance that exists completely to fill the universe, was molded by Mind into all the varying forms that we see around us. The whole universe is a living presence, a spiritual system existing for one thing and one thing alone: to fully express the Divine. God expresses as we grow. Spirit wants a larger, fuller expression in every one of us. Spirit never hinders us; our own limited fear thought is the only thing that can possibly hinder us or keep us from enjoying the largest measure of happiness, health and success. We must grasp this marvelous truth, because it is the only reality. We must throw off all the false beliefs that enslave the world.

The world is deluded, blind and shackled. And by what? By its own acceptance of negative thought. It lies bound in chains of its own forging. Mind, which is our greatest gift, has been made our jailer, and we whimper in a misery entirely of our own creation. *Bondage exists nowhere in the universe except in the mind of human beings,* and freedom is ours at the precise moment we recognize our liberty and step forth as free people.

It is as though we had been incarcerated in a cell for forty years.

Even though the door was now to be left unlocked, we would not make the effort to walk out free. The door that has held your mentality in prison for all these years is at this very moment open, and you are free to claim all the liberty you can enjoy. *But you must make the move for yourself.* No one else can make it for you. No one else can grow for you. You must grow in knowledge yourself.

Those of us who step out into the liberty of our true selves can be certain that we need never again be bound under the old, false belief. We now have a law by which to control our own thinking and, therefore, our own circumstances. This law was always there for us and will always be there, awaiting our direction and carrying out our mental images. The whole universe is a perfect mold of thought and is thought-formed, and our little world is molded by our thought, for better or worse.

Those of us who absorb these lessons and so move upward and forward into a true understanding of our real nature can look back and see ourselves as ones awakened from a nightmare that still holds millions of people in its grasp.

Doubts Must Be Reasoned Away

Some will ask, "What are you to do when doubts creep in? I can accept the fact that I am perfect with divine perfection, but when I try to affirm it, doubts assail me. My own straitened circumstances or my poor health confront me, and I find it difficult to see just one picture: that of perfection."

This is where our reasoning faculties come in. Earlier we said that objective mind in us corresponds to Spirit in the God-head. Spirit has the ability to choose. So we reason with ourselves. We may say, "Since I am the offspring of God, I know that I am as free as God is. I don't care what my feelings are. I deny the reality of those feelings. If my mind were put out of action by an anesthetic, I could not feel this distress. It is only my mind telling me of this pain. I therefore direct my mind to close itself to any belief in pain or distress. Disease is neither person, place nor thing. No place was ever made for it in my body. It has no right there. It is a squatter, and I order it out. It is the result of a false mental picture, and I now affirm the true mental picture and instruct subjective mind to pay attention only to the truth, the wholeness that I now affirm."

⁓

Meditation

I know that within me is the idea of the perfection that is my birthright. I know that now I am a child of God and that as God's child I am not subject to any disease or limitation. All that the Creator has is mine. I therefore receive with rejoicing this fullness of health, freedom from pain and amplitude of supply. There is nothing in me that doubts or disbelieves. It is done unto me as I believe, and because I believe, I accept my good and give thanks for it.

⁓

Questions

1. How can you use imagination to improve your circumstances?
2. Can we consider money to be a spiritual idea?
3. Is it wrong to expect abundance?
4. What keeps us from fuller self-expression?
5. Where does bondage exist?

Answers

1. You should fill your imagination with pictures that embody your desire and free your mind from negative or opposing ideas.
2. Spirit is the ultimate source of all things. Therefore, our financial conditions as well as our bodily and mental conditions have their

origin in Spirit.

3. Objective person is a manifestation of the universal desire for self-expression. Anything that will enlarge the individual's capacity for self-expression must be in line with the universal urge.

4. We are kept from the fuller expression of our God-nature by our mistaken conviction that God expects most of us to be failures, sick and unhappy.

5. Bondage exists only in the mind of humankind. We can be free as soon as we recognize that there is no power to bind us except ourselves.

How to Use the Law of Mind

∽

One of the weaknesses of many of these kinds of teachings or subjects is that they are composed of generalities, which, though excellent, nevertheless fail to meet our actual needs because they do not place in our hands a definite technique for treating ourselves or others. Since this book is intended to enable you definitely and finally to improve your condition and to change your environment, we feel that you should have careful, detailed instructions regarding the exact method to follow in setting the law of Mind into activity.

A prayer treatment is not a mere wish that something better will come into the life. It is not "concentration" on a picture mentally formed, depending for its manifestation on the strength of will accompanying it. It is not just a vague thought sent out into the air to wander aimlessly through space. It is not what is commonly known as "holding a thought," "going into the silence," or engaging in any curious or occult practices whatsoever.

A prayer treatment in Science of Mind is a definite, specific movement of thought in a specific direction to produce in Mind a specific result. There is nothing mysterious about it. It can be done by anyone who wishes, for anyone or any condition. It merely follows clearly defined laws of cause and effect, and it is based on sound, scientific principles of thought action.

The first thing you must keep in mind is that in prayer treatment for others you do not send your thought into another person's mentality. *You treat yourself.* The treatment begins and ends within your own consciousness. You treat to heal yourself of the false belief in the reality of the condition from which the other person is suffering.

We Are Forever Perfect

We start with the fundamental fact that since all people are expressions of God, we all must be and are potentially perfect; that we at our center are the image and likeness of God. Therefore, the inner spiritual self is never sick, sinning, unhappy or limited in any way. True, the outer physical person, the envelope in which the spiritual person dwells, may show evidence of sickness, sin, unhappiness or limitation, but the outer, morbid condition is no more a part of the real person than our clothes are. These conditions can be changed just as clothes can be, without affecting the inner person. But the laws of thought show that the *outer is changed from the inner*, never the reverse.

As long as we believe in the reality of the outer imperfection, we perpetuate it. Race thought and mass thought are a burden on the human race in their false belief that these outer things are real. We go beyond this outer and insist that the inner spiritual perfection is the only reality. We do not spend time dwelling on the false picture of imperfection. We observe it in passing so that we know what we are treating or praying for, but we spend our time during prayer, or treatment, in erasing this picture of the outer imperfection and healing ourselves of the false belief that the human race has accepted concerning its reality. The treatment, then, is for the purpose of convincing ourselves of the fact that we are pure spiritual substance—in our body, our finances, our material affairs of all kinds—and we treat ourselves to know that we are perfect *now*.

Since there is only one Mind, it follows in logical sequence that what is known at one point in Mind must be known at all points. Therefore, the clear, steady, *single image* held by the practitioner of the divine perfection of the client will be made manifest in the outer condition of the person thus seen.

Mind Holds No Conflicting Thoughts

Our distorted material condition is the result of our inner thought distortion. Since it is impossible for Mind to hold two conflicting thoughts, we know that our disturbed mental state, which tells us we are sick, unhappy, poor, etc., cannot possibly be the real one. Therefore, this bad condition has no law to support it and must fall to the ground in the face of the truth that we are perfect. As the practitioner achieves a steady, sure certainty of the perfect condition being treated for, it comes into manifestation. However, if those being treated refuse to admit the truth of the treatment, they shut themselves off from the manifestation of their own innate divinity. Even Jesus could do no mighty works in Nazareth "because of their unbelief."

The Obedience of Subjective Mind

At the outset of a prayer, or treatment, practitioners must have no doubts regarding the responsiveness of the great ocean of subjective mind. We must know beyond the shadow of a doubt that we are surrounded by a neutral, plastic medium that receives the impress of our thought and proceed immediately to carry out this thought. We must have clearly established in our own mind the fact that this great ocean of Mind, which has all power to create anything that we decide, is completely dedicated to our service as though we were the only person in the universe, and this willing servant waits at our elbow to hear our spoken word and swing into action on our behalf.

Complete Relaxation

This knowledge in itself will tend to give us the freedom from strain that is essential when praying. We must be completely relaxed, free from any sense of responsibility for the result. If we have missed this truth, there is a tendency for us to become strained and tense, which is fatal to proper treatment. You must realize that the responsibility for healing the condition is not yours. You are responsible only for setting the law of Mind into activity; Universal Mind is the final healer.

Just as a word spoken into a microphone is taken up, magnified thousands of times by the power of the broadcasting station and sent out to the far corners of the earth, so your word and your thought are taken up by Universal Mind, whose power guides the stars in their courses and is made part of the great cosmic creative system that produces in your client that which was spoken by an ordinary person in an ordinary voice. Loud, tensed shrieking would hinder. Quiet, relaxed confidence produces the proper result, because "It is neither by might nor by power, but by my Spirit, says the Lord."

Unify with the Presence

Once we have gained a clear recognition of this surrounding, obedient ocean of Mind, we must clearly understand our relationship to it. We should make ourselves certain that this ocean of Mind is not something of a different nature from our own mind. We should take time to rid ourselves of all the ideas of the old psychology that there are as many "minds" as there are individuals. Knowing that there is only one Mind, we come to the place where we see and "feel" that our individual mind is merely a small portion of this great Mind that we are able to use. Moreover, we should bring ourselves to the point where we clearly understand that the mind of our client is not something separate, but is merely some part of the ocean of Mind in which the client is thinking.

God's Mind Is Always Perfect

Since Universal Mind, our own mind and the client's mind are all one, just as the several drops of water are all one with the ocean, we are able to understand that the client's apparent condition is merely a negative thought-form. It cannot be reality, because Universal Mind and the practitioner's mind are opposed to it. So the person who is praying turns away from the negative thought-form of the client to the perfect thought-form of the subjective ocean. Unified with this perfect thought-form, we are seeing the client with the eyes of God. If humankind looks on the outward appearance, but God looks on the heart, then humankind sees the miserable exterior condition, but the practitioner sees the divine inner perfection.

God sees nothing that is unlike God. Therefore, in looking at defeated humankind, God does not see defeated human beings. God sees reigning people, unsick, unsinning, happy, well-supplied and healthy. The world labors continually under a burden of false belief in sickness, poverty and misery. This does not mean that people only "imagine" they have trouble. Their troubles are genuine experiences, but are produced by a false view of themselves. We may scream in terror during a nightmare—it is a real mental experience—but on awakening, we know that it had no basis in reality.

The Heart of Treatment

The high point of a treatment is that in which you come into a quiet realization of the truth of what you are saying. You might be treating for financial success, and when you arrive at the point in your thought where there is no longer anything in your mentality that denies the truth that you are affirming, you have reached the peak of the treatment.

It is somewhat difficult to outline the exact point at which perfect realization occurs, but as long as doubts float up into the consciousness, as long as there is not that quiet inner conviction of accomplishment, you may be sure that you have not arrived at the stage of compete realization. Yet somewhere during a treatment, this inner sense of calm arrives, a quiet recognition that what you have been saying about yourself or another *is true*, and there is no longer any need for you to bring up arguments to prove the perfection of the one being treated. In other words, *you know the eternal truth of your words.* When this moment arrives, you are ready to make another move equally important and too frequently neglected by the student.

Let Go and Let God

A good treatment should build up to the point where it can safely and wholeheartedly be released into Mind. This is where our treatment differs from those systems that consist in "holding a thought."

The first part of a treatment is for the purpose of convincing the one treating. That is, since the person being treated "was from the beginning, is now and ever shall be perfect," we have to bring our mentality to the point where it accepts this with no mental reservations whatsoever. Having done this and thereby having brought our mind into oneness with Divine Mind so that there is no conflict at all, we say, "I now release this picture, this knowledge of truth, into Divine Mind, knowing that it is carrying this picture into complete manifestation." Having done so, we turn away from it. It is now in the stage of magnification, as the word spoken into the microphone. The servant, mighty subjective mind, now has it and is working it into form.

Holding On Shows Imperfect Realization

When we find ourselves unable to let go of a treatment, it shows that we have not yet surrendered it to the subjective mind. We are trying to do the work ourselves or to give it a little push, as it were. We must change our attitude and know we have missed the truth that the law of Mind does the work. Our part is merely to recognize the effortless ability of the law to correct this condition, then, having treated *ourselves* to believe implicitly in the working of the law, to release this situation to the mighty law and rest quietly in the assurance that "a greater than Moses is here."

This is a highly important part of truth. You should ponder this diligently until you are sure of yourself, because at this point you must stay in the middle of the road. Others, failing to catch the distinction between their efforts and law's working, have wandered into disillusionment and discouragement. Your strength of will is never going to heal a single soul. All your reading and knowledge, all you "understanding" will never budge one obstacle unless it is seen at its true worth and in its true place. What we do in our own thought activity is merely what the starter does in the automobile. It does not pull the auto along the highway; it merely gives the impetus that starts the mighty motor into action. Then, all the hidden power lying in that motor moves the tons of automobile swiftly, surely and effortlessly to its destination.

∽

Meditation

"Be therefore perfect even as your Creator which is in heaven is perfect." I believe that the Spirit within me is the Spirit of God. Since this is so, my inner nature must be perfect. Instead of contemplating the imperfections of experience, I dwell on this inner perfection. As I contemplate it, I sense an expansion of the perfect and the withdrawal of the imperfect, until my life corresponds outwardly to the inner perfection of the eternal Spirit within me.

∽

Questions

1. What is "treatment" in the Science of Mind?
2. What is the fundamental premise in treatment?
3. What attitudes of mind are helpful in making treatment successful?
4. Does God see "evil"?
5. What is the high point of a treatment?

Answers

1. Treatment is the art and science of directing thought to produce specific results for oneself or for another. It begins and ends in one's own consciousness.
2. The fundamental premise in treatment is that we, each being an expression of God, are potentially perfect. The purpose of a treatment is to convince ourselves that this perfection exists right now.
3. A recognition of the absolute obedience of subjective mind and freedom from tenseness and a sense of responsibility are necessary attitudes of mind in giving treatments.
4. God, being good and being all, sees only good and perfection.
5. The high point of a treatment is when we come to a quiet realization of the absolute truth of our statements.

How to Remove Hindrances

⌒

The beginner in the Science of Mind philosophy—and even those who have a thorough knowledge of the technique—is at times greatly puzzled by specific situations that may arise. This is illustrated by the following incident.

A young man who had commenced to practice this constructive method of thought approached us with this question. He said, "I know that my inner thought life reflects itself in my outer conditions, and I have been endeavoring to change my thought-pattern so as to produce more desirable things for myself. I clearly know what I should do and try to do it. I try to fill my mind with positive images, but in spite of myself I find that the years of negative thought have created habits that draw the negative into my consciousness, even when I am in the midst of quiet meditation, and I don't know how to drive them out."

Sooner or later all students have this experience, and if they are not carefully instructed, they are liable to give up after several futile efforts "to drive out the negative thoughts." Then they conclude either that they are "born in sin" and that this is their old "Adam nature," or else that they have not the necessary "willpower" to carry them to the higher levels of thought. Nothing could be further from the truth. The Science of Mind philosophy can be practiced by anyone, because it does not depend on strong willpower, salvation or anything else except a knowledge of mental law.

You will recall that in our section on objective mind, we brought out the fact that the prime function of subjective mind is to obey and to carry out the orders of objective mind. The prime function of objective mind is to reason, choose and direct subjective mind.

Importance of the Power of Choice

The word *choose* is one of the important words in this study. Every advance that has ever been made by a human beings has been accomplished by a series of cold, conscious, deliberate choices, regardless of the way any individual has felt. The feeling life and the reasoning life are in conflict during the early days when one is taking up the Science of Mind, just as they are during childhood.

Children always want to follow their feelings. Child training is the process of substituting reason for desire. Children want to spend every penny they get for treats, but through reason they are taught the desirability of saving a portion for other things. Their feelings carry children out into the make-believe life, but reason brings them to *choose* the study hours. Athletes are human and occasionally like to go out for a good time, eating anything they wish to the point of excess, keeping late hours, etc. But reason tells them they must consciously *choose* a different course if they are to win a championship. Desire tugged at young Walter Chrysler when the other boys in his little Kansas town were playing during the long evening hours, but *choice* led him to spend long nights learning how to dissect a locomotive. In every pubic library in the land and in evening courses of study are people who have deliberately *chosen* to do the thing they know will mean more to them later on.

Controlling Thought

Only children and savages live under the control of their feelings. Intelligent people live under the dictation of their reasoned choices. Since you have voluntarily *chosen* to study this Science, it is clear that you are one of those on the higher levels of intelligence and therefore able to see what is meant when we refer to advances being made by choice.

Most people get headaches at some time or another. Those who live by their feelings use this as an excuse for letting down in their endeavor. Those who live by their *choices* go on in spite of their headaches and do great things. "We cannot keep the birds from flying over our heads, but we can prevent them from building nests in our hair." We cannot prevent negative thoughts from seeking an outlet in our consciousness, but we can *choose* to admit only those that we desire.

You should remember that thoughts never come singly, but in pairs, because one is always the reverse of the other. Whenever a negative thought comes to the mind, remember that no thought can force its way in until it is permitted. So just say, "I refuse that negative idea and accept its positive opposite, which I know is there with it." We may think that we do not choose the thoughts that we entertain, but that is because a lifetime of negative thinking has made the choosing of the negative an automatic thing.

Subjective Mind Responds

At first, the process of refusing the negative and deliberately choosing the positive will have to be more or less of a conscious activity, just as the formation of any new mental habit has to be. The subjective acceptance of the negative has been going on for years, but it is a completely submissive servant, caring not whether it accepts negative or positive, and it will uncomplainingly swing around in time under the direction of the objective mind's choice until you will find it easier and easier to keep your thinking on a constructive level. The activity of the subjective mind is completely reversible. It can be educated to follow any thought pattern you decide to set. Just as the sunflower follows the sun, when you turn, subjective mind will turn.

Let us suppose that you have decided to manifest more prosperity. The past pattern has been one of want, debt, fear. Your conversation or your thought in the past has been, "I have so many bills to pay. I am late with the butcher. I wish I had more money. I hate rich people who have no worries like mine. It's tough to be poor, and I don't suppose it will ever be any different for me." This is a typical thought-pattern in such a case, and the subjective has fully absorbed it. By this continual contemplation of lack and poverty, you have tended to produce it because you have drawn this mighty law of Mind into continuing the thing you are contemplating.

But we have decided to change all this. We now see that we are one with all the good in the universe. Instead of envying or hating successful people, we rejoice with them, because we recognize that they have drawn a large or a steady supply from the one source. We know that they have no private access to the source which is denied us, and the fact that they have it is proof that we too may have it. Since they are one with us, we have had a share in that draft on the Infinite Bank.

We know that we are Spirit in origin and that Spirit cannot be poor. Therefore, neither can we be poor unless we set the law to making or keeping us poor. We recognize the fact that money is a spiritual thing, spiritually conceived; that as soon as we get the inner consciousness of money, we will have the outer refection or extension of this thought that is material money. We realize that Spirit can never be limited in any way, nor can it be kept back from having anything that it wants. Since we are Spirit, there is nothing limiting us *except our own thought*.

Knowing this, we begin to affirm and to *know* within ourselves that we have all things. We begin to ponder the richness of the Infinite, the fullness of supply that streams toward us from the inexhaustible reservoir of the universe. We see ourselves one with it, and we proclaim as we turn away from the contemplation of our past lack, "I have all and abound. All supply is mine right now." Immediately the negative thought pops up, "You certainly don't look it. You look like a pauper to me." This is the very moment when we *choose* to know that, in spite of all outward appearances, *we are prosperous,* because riches within will produce riches without. So we say, "I've listened to lies long enough, and they have only brought me misery. Right now I deny those false beliefs and affirm the truth. I am prosperous. I am prosperous because *I choose to know* that I am prosperous." It is important that you catch this fine distinction between the choosing life and the feeling life, because it is the crux of the problem in making your move from the place were you are to the place where you want to be.

Mental Equivalents

The question is frequently raised, "Why do some people get more than others?" It is sometimes asked in a querulous manner, as though the universe is unfair. The underlying assumption in such a case is that God has responded to some with a greater gift than to others. Those who get more do so not because God has responded to their prayers more than to others, but because they have responded more to God's mental law than others have.

Since Mind is the only actor, cause, and power that there is, the measure of our thought must certainly be the measure of our accomplishment. Water will rise to its own level, and all the praying in the world will not cause it to rise one-thousandth of an inch above that level. So manifestation will be at the exact level of our thought. If we want a sure index of the measure of our hidden thought-life, we can get it accurately by seeing what we are bringing into our outer life.

If we are manifesting peace, happiness, health, prosperity, friends and all other good things of life, then that is what the inner thought-life must be originating. If we are manifesting worry, confusion, bitterness, lack, sickness, loneliness, then that is what the inner life originates. We had better be honest with ourselves in this matter, because it is the gateway through which we will pass into the abundant life. There is no other way through, around or over the wall; we must go through the gate.

The whole teaching of Jesus appears to have been based on the truth that we are surrounded by an intelligent law that does unto each of us *as we believe*. It is measured unto us according to our own measuring. If our belief is limited, our demonstration will be limited. If it is ordinary, the manifestation will be ordinary. If great and superlative, the demonstration will be great and superlative. This is called the law of mental equivalents.

Action Is in the Mind

Jesus not only believed that there was something in the law of the universe that would respond to him, but what is more important, *he had the mental equivalent of its response in his consciousness.* The law of Mind is infinite and perfect, but in order to make a demonstration we must have the mental equivalent of the thing we desire. A demonstration, like anything else in the objective life, is born from a mental concept. The mind is the fashioning factor, and its range, vision and positiveness will reflect itself in the resulting circumstance or experience

For example, if you see only unloveliness in others, it is because unloveliness is a strong element in you. The light you throw on others is in your own soul, and you see others as you *choose* to see them. You hold constantly in your own mind a mental equivalent of unloveliness and create unlovely reactions toward yourself. You are getting back what you are sending out. If you believe yourself to be a failure and that it is useless for you to try to be anything else, you carry *with and within yourself* the mental equivalent of failure. So you succeed in being a failure according to law. Even this failure is a demonstration.

Those who understand the systematic use of the law will understand that if they are failing, they are *where* they are because of *what* they are. So we will begin to disclaim what we *appear* to be and affirm what we *know* ourselves actually to be. As our statements dissolve wrong subjective tendencies, providing in their place a correct concept of life and reality, we will automatically be lifted out of our failure. Impelling forces sweeping everything before us will set us free if we trust in Spirit and *accept* the working of the law.

∽

Meditation

Humankind is God in manifestation, the out-picturing of an eternal thought in the mind of God. God's pictures are always complete and perfect, beautifully painted and thoroughly satisfying. Now I know that I am such an outpicturing of Spirit. There is in me no imperfection, because I am a representation of a perfect original, a unique manifestation of the Divine Mind. I deliberately erase from my thought every belief in limitation, condemnation or fear. I announce my perfect freedom from every restricting idea, and I permit pure life to flow through me. My every act proclaims my harmony with the God within. Thus my inner life becomes the pattern for my outward expression, and there wells up within me a consciousness of a deep and abiding peace, the peace of God.

∽

Questions

1. How can we control thought?
2. How does the subjective mind react to the images of thought presented to it?
3. What would be the result of constantly thinking of lack?
4. Why do some people have more than others?
5. What do we mean by "mental equivalents?"

Answers

1. We control thought by our power of choice. We can deliberately refuse to entertain negative thoughts and choose the type of thought we will permit to function through us.
2. The subjective mind reacts automatically to the images of thought presented to it, whether they are negative or positive. It is always the responsive servant, not arguing, only doing.
3. The final result of dwelling on lack would be to experience poverty.
4. Their abundance is due to their more positive receptivity and acceptance of supply in response to mental law.
5. By "mental equivalents" we mean the subjective idea of a desired experience. As we improve our inner vision, there is a corresponding improvement in experience.

The Value of Prayer

⚮

The student who has followed carefully along thus far might be pardoned for asking the question, "Does this Science believe there is any value in prayer?"

The Science of Mind teaches that there is very great efficacy in prayer. While it is true that the law which creates is impersonal, God is more than the law. God is Spirit, absolute and unconditioned, but individualized in the consciousness of the individual. So we should not allow ourselves to swing over to the extreme of believing that we live in a universe that is nothing but the operation of one big law. This at best would be a very cold, cheerless philosophy.

What Is Prayer?

We are definitely opposed to the old idea of prayer, which was a series of pleadings to a capricious God who might or might not grant us our desires. This old idea was coupled with a sort of moral policing that taught that there were certain "sins" that militated against the possibility of receiving answers to prayer. These were practices of a moral nature or habits that were generally frowned upon in theological circles. Some of them were fairly harmless, such as card playing, theater-going and dancing, but others involved habits such as liquor and tobacco.

We believe that the individual is the best judge of the desirability of these things and that if anyone finds any personal habit or practice that clouds their vision of reality, it should be dropped from their life, because anything that hinders one from forming full mental equivalents will, to the same degree, hinder the law from creating complete manifestations for them. But it is a matter of personal growth, not in any way connected with a divine police officer.

We do not believe in praying for a thing and using the argument that we will use it for a good purpose if we get it. The law knows only to create according to the mental equivalent, and it will not work any more swiftly because we want to do good with the answer

We do not believe in praying for something because we are in such want and must have it. It is true that we pray for things we must have, but the world is full of people who want and need things yet never get them because they have never built up the proper mental equivalent.

We *do* pray with a quiet, calm, assured confidence that we can have anything that we can mentally accept; that the law immediately swings into action to that end; that it will create for us that which we know we can have. We do not pray with the proviso "give us this if it is God's will for us to have it," because we believe that since it is God's nature to express, it must be God's will to give us anything that contributes to our growth, happiness and fullness without being harmful to someone else.

Fundamental Harmony of the Universe

There is a fundamental harmony in the universe. The same law that operates for me also operates for my neighbor. It would wreck itself and the universe if it could create something for me by taking away from my neighbor, because then, while giving to me, it could not be an obedient, all-producing law for my neighbor.

Mind creates for us out of the great reservoir of the unformed spiritual substance. It never has to take from anyone, because it has unlimited raw material on which to draw. Therefore, it is not necessary for my neighbors to be made poor so that I can have their substance with which to become rich. There is plenty to make everyone rich and satisfied.

If my happiness must be gained by bringing sorrow to another, I must in my illumination forego any desire to have that thing. If I should persist in trying to get it, by the same law that I would get it, I would lose it. If I cause my neighbor's tears to flow, then by the same law my tears will be made to flow. If I bring sorrow into the life of another, then into my life will sorrow be brought.

True students of Science of Mind want no good brought to themselves that they do not want brought to others. That which we wish for ourselves, we must wish for all others, because everyone is an expression of the one God. We don't want a new Mercedes so that we can outshine our neighbor with a broken bicycle. Recognizing the fundamental harmony of the universe and the universal family of humankind, we "rejoice with them that do rejoice."

Prayer Is Accepting, Not Pleading

True prayer is based on a faith that is scientific. *Scientific faith is an attitude of mind that is so convinced of its own idea and so completely accepts it that any contradiction is unthinkable and impossible.* The student should memorize this definition.

Our faith is based on:

1. The all-power of the law. We are convinced that Mind has all intelligence, all ability, all power, all wisdom, and knows how to create anything that is created. We can think of the most difficult thing it is possible for our finite mind to imagine and can rest in the assurance that Mind knows how to solve that problem or to create a new condition;

2. The absolute obedience of the law to our will. The law never reasons with us, saying, "I don't think that would be a good thing for you to have";

3. The undeviating neutrality of the law. The law has no preferences. It never draws back and says, "That goes against the grain with me." It is absolutely neutral. If it could talk to us, it would say, "You go ahead and name it, and I'll make it." It doesn't make one kind of thing better than another. It is willing to create whatever we dictate. In fact, *the law is not a person*; it is an intangible principle of Mind that operates in this unswerving, obedient way because it is its nature to do so.

The law obeys us when we recognize its mode of action. When we understand that objective mind in us corresponds to Spirit in the Godhead, we know that we must reason objectively and decide exactly what we want. Then when we speak our word, it is the word of Spirit, which the law always obeys. We rise far above the idea of a puny person standing upright and calling on the Great Creative Mind to do our bidding. Being the expression of God, when we speak our word, that word becomes the word of God to the law. Thus you can see why we release the thought. We don't keep clinging to it. God spoke, and it was done. We speak as Spirit, and if our mental equivalent is on the level of our word, it is done.

Exactness in Prayer

A prayer must include within itself *everything* that we want the answer to contain. We must remember that the law does not reason. It does not put in extra things that we forgot or take out things that we did not notice were harmful. It takes *exactly* what we put in our mental equivalent, and this alone is what it creates. Some time ago, a woman told us that all her life she had wanted a home with beautiful grounds. She came to a California city and treated that she would demonstrate just such a home. Within two months, she found at a bargain price exactly what she wanted:

fourteen rooms, acres of grounds in lawn, flowers and fruit trees, rambling old stables with servant quarters above them, and all in the most delightful setting. But she had never thought of putting into her prayer the idea of sufficient income to take care of all this. The water bill alone was sufficient to stagger her, and before many months, she gave up the effort and moved out. The law of Mind will give us just as much as we include in our directions to it, no more and no less.

Another woman had a bookstore, but few people came in. She decided to treat for more activity. She prayed along this line and built up her mental picture of crowds of people coming in and out of her store. The law swung into action and the crowds came, but she had omitted the thought that those who would come would appreciate her goods, want to buy them, have the money to buy them and *would* buy them. She failed to hear the cash register ring often, to see the customers smiling as she wrapped their books and handed them over while they handed over their money to her.

The crowds handled her books, which became shopworn and of decreased value. She was in despair when we suggested that the law was giving her just what she had asked for: activity. Fortunately, she profited by the advice and followed the suggestion that she add these other ideas to her treatment. The result? Good crowds, good business and good financial returns.

Answer to Prayer Is in the Prayer

When a prayer or treatment is released, it is a completed thing. It is now in the hands of the law and will be carried forward into manifestation just as it is. Those who speak their word and release their desire, but are filled with doubt and misgiving as to whether they will ever be answered, have answered it right there, because the prayer will be answered but in reverse. *All prayers are answered,* although not always in the way we would like. They are answered according to what is in the mind of the individual at the time.

If our prayers are released, as Jesus' were with the fullest confidence that the law can do nothing else but answer them, our demonstrations will come thick and fast. If they are sent out with only partial acceptance, then they will be only partially answered. If with little or no inward conviction, then the answer will be of a like nature. There is no escape from this and no exception. Remember, we are dealing with inexorable law that never deviates and never varies. *It knows only to obey.*

The Law Works for Anyone

This law of Mind is impersonal, like the law of electricity that will move into action for anyone who observes the principles governing its flow. An Einstein or an ignorant Hottentot may press the button. The electricity doesn't care who it is, because it is its nature to flow at the touch of that button. Even the tiny fingers of a three-year-old child may set it into action. There is only one prerequisite: *The button making the connection must be pushed.* So the law of Mind flows always in the direction of constructive creative activity when we understand and apply the principles by which it works. You have the mightiest force in all the world to command. You are now stepping out of the prison of ignorance and fear, into the light of a constructive expectancy that will re-make your world for you.

The Attitude of Rejoicing

In releasing our word into the universal subjectivity, we do so with a glad and thankful heart. Giving thanks is a further indication that we have fully released our word. It means that we are sure of the completion of the creative process; that there are no lingering doubts. Those who are still unconvinced do not rejoice; they wait until they see if it is going to work. But if you have done the work thoroughly and well, you can turn your back on that particular treatment, give thanks for its certainty and rejoice in its fulfillment even though you have not seen it outwardly fulfilled as yet. So, we "rejoice evermore."

∞

Meditation

There is only one Mind, one life, one truth, one intelligence, which is over all, in all, pervading all and able to recognize itself in all. This Mind appreciates itself in its manifestation in every form and every person. This Mind is my mind and is the reality of my being, its source and its continuance. This Mind is also the mind of everyone with whom I am in any way associated. Therefore, there is an immediate understanding of everything I do or say.

There is in me no fear, no confusion, no apprehension, no disturbance. There is in me only a spirit of peace, of understanding and of goodwill. I know that there is nothing in the world that can harm me and no one who wishes to do me any injury. The voice in me is the voice of God. My word is the word of God. The result of that word is perfection, happiness, stability, security. There is nothing in the universe that can hinder this word, disturb it, frustrate it or deflect it. Nothing can take place except perfect action, satisfying, complete and full. This right action is now and always will be operative in all my affairs.

∞

Questions

1. What should our attitude be toward personal habits such as smoking, drinking, etc.?
2. What should be our interpretation of "God's will"?
3. Would it do any good to plead with God for something that we desire?
4. What is the basis of our faith?

5. Does God ever play favorites?

Answers

1. Our personal habits are primarily our own affair, but anything that would bring hurt to ourselves or another, or would blur our mental vision, should be dropped from our lives.
2. As long as what we desire will bring no harm to anyone else and will enrich our own experience, it cannot be opposed to the will of God. It is the nature of God to express. It follows that the will of God and the nature of God are one.
3. True prayer is not pleading, because God is always good. True prayer is accepting the desired condition as already here.
4. Our faith is based on a belief in an impersonal but intelligent law that is responsive to our word. God is no respecter of persons.
6. Anyone can use the law. We do not attempt to manipulate God; we use impersonal law.

THE WILL AND THE IMAGINATION

You should by this time be getting clear insight into the reasons why conditions are changed through proper vision and understanding. Science of Mind, breaking away as it does from many commonly accepted notions, parts company with the world's belief when it comes to the comparative value of the will and the imagination.

From earliest times, people have worshipped at the shrine of the will. They have bowed to stronger wills and have sought to develop greater willpower within themselves so that others might be brought under their domination. They have assumed that in some strange way willpower must be tied in with their getting what they want from life. And if they have felt themselves to be lacking in this mysterious "willpower," they have often become discouraged and have given up seeking to mold their own affairs.

Some years ago, a violinist in a leading symphony orchestra came in with this problem. He said, "I have studied the violin from childhood. My technique has been commended by masters as perfect, and I love music with all my soul. I do my work in the orchestra without any sense of mental strain, apart from the normal exertion called for in playing. But when I am called on to take a solo part, I am miserable and unhappy. It is extreme punishment for me. I can execute my work perfectly at home, but something happens inside me at the public performance. I get panicky. I have tried to force myself to get over this feeling. I have gone out of my way to try to develop my willpower, as suggested by others, but it is of no use. Am I doomed for life by this nervousness, or is there any way that I can get over it?"

To go the end of this incident before taking up the method used, let me say that this musician learned a truth that he since reported has changed his whole outlook on life, as well as made it possible for him to do the most intricate solo work without the slightest mental disturbance.

Willpower Is Not the Strongest Power

To begin with, willpower is not humankind's strongest force. The imagination is far more potent that the will and, when properly understood, is the directing force behind the will, giving will all its drive.

Going back into the history of the human race, the imagination is much older than the will. Long before human beings even knew they had a will, they were exercising their imagination. Before their will and reason had worked out any system of letters, they were tracing figures on the walls of caves. Their imaginations were seeking to transfer images of other living things from their immaterial word to the material world of their abode. In fact, the first ancestor of humans who rose from a position on all fours to stand erect on hind legs did so through the power of imagination, not will.

In the history of humankind, the imagination is older than the will. A child, in its personal evolution, passes through the stage of imaginative development long before the will has become active. The story-telling age, the age at which a broomstick becomes a horse to a child, is long past by the time reason and will develop.

Since imagination is older than will, it follows that it is more deeply seated in consciousness than is the will, and a logical corollary of this is that imagination is far stronger than will. Therefore, in any conflict between the imagination and the will, the imagination is bound to win. This is exemplified in the case of trying to stop blushing or bursting into tears. The sense of shame or loss pictured by the imagination is so vivid that, try as we may, we find it difficult to exercise sufficient willpower to check its effect. We may say, "I know I'm a silly fool to give way like this, but I just can't help it!" Imagination is stronger than will

We may be perfectly able to talk intelligently and naturally to others or in a small group of friends, but when asked to speak on a platform to perhaps only twenty people, we are gripped by a horrible fear and say, "Oh, I cannot speak in public!" Anyone who can talk to one person can be a public speaker, if not an orator, unless they allow their imagination to stop them. What really happens is that our imagination, which is simply our ability to "image," builds up pictures of ourselves stuttering and stammering, or people scorning or criticizing us, and this image of failure is so active that we find ourselves unable to overcome it through our will. In the Science of Mind, we make use of imagination to help us rise to the heights, whereas uninstructed people use it to pull them down to the depths.

Habits

Those trying to break destructive habits or build constructive new habits through willpower will find that they can solve their habit problem through the right use of the imagination. Depending on will alone, they resolve to break a habit, grit their teeth and "swear off," only to find that they have exhausted their energy in doing this. Then the imagination commences to build seductive pictures of the great pleasure connected with the performance of the habit, and although the will feebly protests, the imagination carries them over again into the habit.

Why Imagination Is Potent

The power of the imagination lies in the fact that is the *creative* activity. As stated earlier, creative activity follows vision. In the beginning of any creative series, God contemplates the image of that which God desires to create, and it manifests because any image steadily contemplated is bound to manifest. We likewise hold an image and then superimpose on it another conflicting image, and both tend to come forth, but neither one clear and sharp. Thus the multiplicity of images hinders most people in their quest for progress.

To use your power of imagining correctly, the first thing is to "know the truth" about yourself. This truth is *perfection in every department of your being and activity.* If you have firmly convinced yourself that this is the truth and that all apparent manifestations to the contrary are false, then the next thing is to enlist the imagination on your behalf. All of us have the ability to image. We are constantly imaging something, but in the past it has been failure, sickness, unhappiness and other negative conditions.

Now we have decided that since perfection is the true state and since Spirit regards us always as in a state of perfection, we will likewise take the time to create the proper images of perfection for ourselves. It is not difficult, for instance, to think of perfection in health. Sick people whose contemplation has long been on their own infirmities can quite easily call into their consciousness the image of some acquaintance who is the picture of health. They can think of an infant whose beautiful skin, soft ears and toes betoken perfect health. They can carry this "imaging" further to place themselves in the center of the picture, "imagining" if they haven't courage to merely "image" themselves there, imagining what it would be like to have that bubbling-over health and vitality, the ability to eat and to enjoy all sorts of food, to sleep soundly and awake rested and refreshed. Then they can quietly say to themselves, "I am now expressing the perfection of pure Spirit."

They can go on to argue with their negative mental states that deny this. They can say, "Yes, I know that for years I have not experienced health such as this, but that is because I have believed lies that passed for truth. I have believed the evidence of my senses and have turned the truth of God into a lie. The truth is, I am at this very moment perfect in health. Everything in the universe wishes me to enjoy that health. Sickness is an old superstition that formerly enslaved me. I have now passed from the contemplation of death to the contemplation of life, and I revel in the knowledge that I am free from all false belief in the reality of this which I have been experiencing. I now accept perfection of health as my true state, and this is the image that I release unto Mind to manifest in me and for me."

All of this is done not through will, nor accompanied by a great effort or straining to produce it, but through a quiet process of meditation. The less mental "forcing," the better, because it does not take wrinkled brows and clenched fists to form the picture. Spirit is never strained or tensed. Spirit creates by contemplation, and what it contemplates passes into manifestation.

The public speaker can rest quietly in the knowledge that, "These people want to hear me speak. They like what I have to say and the way I say it. They are hungry for encouragement or illumination on their problems and are looking for me to talk to them as I would if we were sitting at home. I have prepared and have something worthwhile to say, and I know that others want to and will be benefited by what I say."

The orchestra violinist previously mentioned followed such a method of imaging. He laughed at himself for imagining that people were ready to pounce on any possible flaw and told himself that from now on he would imagine the nicest reception, the deafening applause, etc. He reasoned within himself that since his imagination could paint either a friendly or a hostile picture of the audience, he would elect to paint an image of friendliness.

Those seeking freedom from a habit can firmly draw either a picture of the undesirable features of that habit, the details of which present to their imagination an undesirable picture or, on the other hand, a pleasant picture of freedom from the habit with a complete detachment from any response to it.

A student once brought to us the method he used in breaking himself of the habit of smoking. We believe that all people have the right to decide for themselves which habits are desirable and which are a hindrance. This young man decided that he was going to quit smoking. He had tried several times through supreme efforts of will and had never been able to succeed. But after getting this truth about the power of the imagination, he did the following.

He sat down and thought of every single reason he could possibly think of for quitting. Then he said, "I'll make this into a picture and instruct Mind to receive it and to remove all desire for cigarettes."

Then, every time he took out a cigarette, he looked it over and started talking ostensibly to it (but actually to his imagination) in this way: "You are a dirty, disgusting habit. You make me stink to high heaven until my presence is obnoxious to many sensitive people. You use money that I can put to much better use. You have irritated my throat and my nerves. You have not done my digestion any good either.

"I am losing all my desire for you. My inner spiritual self has never had any desire for you, and now my outer physical person has no desire for you either. I am quitting you without effort or struggle. I simply do not respond to your appeal.

"I speak my word to this effect, and my word becomes the law unto this thing. I announce my word into Mind, that cigarettes have not the slightest appeal to me and that I wish to have no response to them, and I now announce that it is done unto me as I believe."

In four days, he had lost all desire for smoking. And three years later, the desire had not returned. This is a concrete illustration of the fact that the imagination is more powerful than the will. This person's will was involved only to the extent that it made the decision to quit. His imagination was then brought into action to paint the picture of his loss of desire or response to the appeal, and the obedient law of Mind did the rest.

Meditation

Jesus told his disciples when they were praying for something to imagine they had it and they would have it. I know that the imagination is the instrument of power and of achievement. Today I resolve to paint mental pictures of only those things that are beautiful and satisfying, and I know that the law will work in response to my imagination to bring into manifestation my heart's desires.

Questions

1. Which is more powerful, the will or the imagination?
2. Why is the imagination more potent?
3. How could imagination be used to improve health?
4. What is the function of the will?
5 What attitude do successful public speakers have?

Answers

1. Imagination is more powerful than the will. It is older than the will and is the directing power behind it.
2. Imagination is more potent because it is a form of creative activity.
3. If we could see ourselves as perfect in our creative imagination, thus inducing in Mind a subjective equivalent of perfect being, our health would automatically improve.
4. The function of the will is to direct the imagination.
5. Successful public speakers know that people wish to hear them speak and enjoy what they have to say and the way they say it.

The Law of Increase

〜

There is a law operative in the universe which is of great value to humankind and which, for convenience's sake, we might call the law of increase. We will first consider how laws are discovered, because if this is clear to you, then you can see the reasons for knowing there is such a thing as the law of increase.

In the field of material science, this is how a law is discovered:

First, someone observes certain phenomena. They see certain results following certain activities. They notice that the same results always follow the same activities, so they assume that these activities are the cause of the results;

Second, they attempt to set this activity into motion. If they obtain the results noted before, they assume that there is some law underlying its activity that assures the result;

Third, they test their theory repeatedly. If they always secure the same results from the same activities, they feel sure of their thesis. So they search out and name their law;

Fourth, they announce their law, and if it is a law, it will respond to the activity initiated by anyone. And it must respond in this inexorable way thousands of times in thousands of attempts, because if one single exception occurs in which it fails so to respond, they may be sure they have not discovered law but merely a coincidence.

This is the way that the laws of gravitation, electricity, aerodynamics, chemical affinity, etc., were discovered. Once the laws are established, they work in America, Africa or Australia, *at the will of the person who understands the law.*

Life Can Never Stand Still

It is a matter of common observation that nothing in life can ever remain static, that is, stand still. Always there is either progression or retrogression. There is evidently a principle of growth and development in the living universe. Everything alive constantly seeks to grow and increase. This is true of the seed. In the earth, it gradually swells, bursts and sends forth a shoot. This makes its way to the surface and emerges into the sunlight. It continues this "increase of cells" and develops more and more until it is a stalk of wheat carrying many more seeds or a tree carrying many seeds. The animal cell does likewise until it is a complete organism carrying many more seeds within its body.

The physical body increases in size and weight without any conscious guidance on the part of the child or animal. It is carried on through the same intelligent law that causes the body of the grain or the tree to increase. Then when the body has reached full stature, growth and increase continue in what we commonly call *ambition.* The mind seeks great achievement, a better home or automobile or business or paycheck. In spiritual things, there is an increasing desire for spiritual unfoldment. These things are an inner urge in humankind that we must either combat and choke down or to which we must give expression, because they are the result of the operation of the law of increase.

Both Good and "Evil" Subject to Law

The condition of the body is never the same for two consecutive seconds. The chemical constituents of your body are not exactly the same as they were when you commenced reading this book. Either the good, true picture (health) has increased or the false picture (disease) has gained. It is the nature of this law constantly to increase that which is the dominant thought-pattern in the consciousness even though we are entirely unconscious of it. It is the nature of Mind always to increase that which is held before it, through its ceaseless creative activity.

Business Subject to Law

No business is in exactly the same financial condition from minute to minute. Either the profits or the losses are constantly increasing. Even though the cash register has not rung for an hour or the bank balance is the same as it was an hour ago, the rent has run on, and also the light bill and the wages of the employees so that the expenses have continued. If new sales are made and more money comes in, then by this same law the profits have increased.

People sometimes say, "Well, I earn the same wages I did last year, so at least I'm holding my own. I am not slipping." This is not true, because the national wealth is increasing every year by a certain percentage. Unless your earning power increases at least by this percentage, you are actually slipping.

Only One Law

The law that underlies the law of increase is the same law that underlies all the life-action in the universe. There are not several "laws," as some think, but only one law. In material science, we have the recent announcement of such a thinker as Einstein, who affirms that there are not several laws of physics, but only one law manifesting itself in multitudinous forms. All other so-called "laws" are only diverse workings of this one great law in the physical universe. Thus modern physics endorses the findings of ancient metaphysics.

Impersonalness of Law

As we studied earlier, the chief characteristic of this law is its utter impersonalness. All law is impersonal. Judges may hold a violent distaste for the color of a litigant's necktie or mannerisms or language, but their decisions must be rendered quite independently of their distaste and must be made in strict accordance with the law as it is written.

Law knows nothing except to act in accord with its own principles. Thus the law of increase becomes to us a law of life or a law of death, of prosperity or of limitation, of happiness or of misery, of health or of sickness, according to the thought-pattern. Strictly speaking, we know that there is no reality in the law of death, limitation, misery or sickness. We merely use these terms for convenience's sake.

But the impersonalness of the law causes it to take *every* thought and attempt to bring it into a manifest form in the outer word. Not only this, but in the phase called the law of increase, it tends to increase every thought to magnify it. Since it has been true from the beginning that everything God created brings forth "according to its own kind," that same thing applies to our thought life.

Jesus said that it was ridiculous to imagine that a thorn bush could produce grapes or a thistle could produce figs. This law of reproduction "after" its kind absolutely precludes it. A pair of dogs cannot produce a litter of kittens, nor can snakes produce birds. We may rest assured that the thought life is no exception. Therefore, we can understand how the person whose mind is occupied with thoughts and fears of sickness will have these thoughts increased until sickness is produced and by the very same law that would just as willingly have produced health.

Those who hold poverty thoughts will increase their poverty, and so on through the entire category of conditions. It is not that God "causes" sickness or poverty, but that a law that was intended for our good has been used for the reverse because of the nature of the things we have contemplated.

We Can Separate Thoughts

Since the tendency of anything sent on its way in life is to increase, it is easy for us to see that our chief responsibility is to *select that which we send into action.* We still hold the steering wheel of our thought-life, and the purpose of "selection" is to separate the worthy from the unworthy, the desirable from the undesirable.

Our Marvelous Power

The power of choice with which we have been endowed is either our greatest blessing or our greatest curse. Properly understood, it can lift us to the heights; misunderstood, it can drag us to the depths. We are free to choose anything that we wish, but we must accept the responsibility for our choices, because inexorable law will make our surroundings according to our choices.

Some years ago, a man tried to do an unfair, unkind thing. He and his wife were separating, and he was sending her out to either starve or get along as best she could. She had moved into a miserable room with her three young children. The divorce laws of that particular state were written in such a way that he could be cruel and unfair if he wished. Because of personal friendship, we tried to persuade the man to do the right thing, but he was adamant. He set his mouth in a straight line and shouted, "Let them starve. I'll make her dance to my tune or else." He had the power to select, and he had selected. What he did not know was that whatever he would select, he would become, or put another way, that his thought was vibrating to that thing. He went on his way clinging to this consuming hate-thought, and by the law of increase his thought was magnified until it literally shook him to pieces mentally. His nerves refused to stand the strain, and he became paralyzed and lay flat on his back for years until death released him. His own power of selection had been used to destroy himself.

Quite the reverse is true when we use our power of selection in a constructive way. When Jesus healed the sick, he consciously selected the thought of the divine perfection. Surrounded even as he was by the complaints, the cries, the vileness, the forms of sickness in others, he withdrew within his own consciousness and there deliberately contacted the divine perfection.

He resolutely closed his mind to the apparent imperfection all around him. He saw God, the all-good. The result of this selection was to raise his thought-level to the God-level. He became the thing he thought. He saw and knew nothing of disease. He consciously saw Spirit unsinning, unsick, whole, vital, harmonious.

Since thoughts are things or vibration, this God-vibration was magnified by the law of increase until it did the very opposite of what was done in the life of the man referred to above. It took the shattered, paralyzed nervous system of the man who lay at the Pool of Siloam, and the constructive change was wrought so that he arose, took up his bed and walked.

The law of increase takes care of that which we have mentally accepted and does it in an entirely neutral, impersonal way. It does not try to punish the one and love the other. It knows only to work and cares not about that on which it works. It is strictly a law of increase.

Speeding Up the Process

The higher the understanding of law and the clearer the illumination of the individual, the more rapidly can the law of increase operate. An example of this is in the matter of the loaves and fishes.

Jesus did not violate any law when he increased these. He merely increased the rate of the process. There is nothing called "time" to Spirit. A day and a thousand years are the very same to eternal Spirit. Jesus saw the whole lengthy process of the grain to the finished loaf in a moment of what we call *time*, because he was thinking the God thought. Therefore, his "miracle" was merely the working of law, timeless and instant, merely the application of higher understanding of the one law.

The same thing happened in his healings, which were instantaneous. We are saturated with the notion that certain diseases take a long time to heal. Jesus wiped out the idea of time. He lived in the *now*. If we had the same consciousness, we could heal just as instantly.

∽

Meditation

I know that there is a law of increase operating through the universe. I see how it multiplies one seed into many seeds so that life may continue to express itself in living forms. I know that when I plant any seed thought in the creative medium of Mind, the law of increase takes it and multiplies it. I now consciously plant the seed thought of those desires whose manifestation will bring abundance into expression for me, and I quietly await the inevitable and joyous harvest.

∽

Questions

1. Does life ever stand still?
2. What causes health and disease?
3. Does the law of increase apply to business?
4. Is there a law of sickness?

5. How do we use this power constructively?

Answers

1. Life never stands still. There is always progression or retrogression, expansion or diminution, in accordance with subjective thought patterns, individual or universal.
2. Health and disease depend on the dominant thought pattern in the consciousness.
3. The law of increase applies to business as well as to health. The dominant thought pattern controls in business. If success is dominant, a person is successful; if fear of failure dominates, then failure is certain.
4. There is only one law, which produces sickness or health, prosperity or adversity, in exact correspondence to the prevailing thought patterns.
5. We use our power constructively by constantly perceiving ourselves as perfect and our affairs as harmonious. As we unify with the one power, it operates through our experience to bring us an expanding good.

The Divine Mental Picture

⟡

How do we know what God's view of us is? And what difference does it make anyway? Is it not better that we should have a correct view of God, rather than try to find out what God's thought of us is? The whole history of evolution in religion, science and philosophy is merely a history of humankind groping after God, using the term *God* from the viewpoint that it means the intelligent life principle, creative imagination and dynamic law in everything, making everything what it is.

From the time human beings first discovered that we were different from the rest of creation—that is, that we were thinkers—we have felt that there must be an infinite Thinker behind all the physical things we could see or touch. As our conception of God has grown, that is, as we have become more conscious of the laws of nature, our understanding of what the nature of God must be has increased. We see intelligence behind everything. We have come a long way in our thinking since the early days in which we imagined God to be an angry deity hurling thunderbolts from the heavens. This childish and grotesque conception of a God whose voice was in the thunder, whose vengeance was seen in the lightning, the earthquake and the flood, has given way to an understanding of the universe as a place of law and order. We now view the terrestrial wonders as natural phenomena, and we no longer believe that the intelligence working in these phenomena carries any thought of anger or punishment.

Disease Is Not Punishment

People used to think of disease and misery as evidence that humanity had incurred the displeasure of God. Now we know that they are merely the logical consequence of our own mistakes. We also know that when we cease making mistakes, the curse is lifted. We know that there is no mystery of suffering any more than there is a mystery of a flat tire after running over a broken bottle. We view things now as definite sequences of cause and effect, and we know that these sequences are operative in the experiences that we call *good* and *evil*. We have come to understand that all the forces of nature are neutral. For instance, water can quench our thirst or drown us. Fire can burn us or cook our food. The same garden plot will bear more than one kind of fruit and vegetation.

Through research and proper interpretation of the laws of thought, we are coming to a more intelligent conception of the nature of God. Since they are as definite as any other laws of nature, and since the movement of thought is mechanical and mathematical, why not understand just what kind of thought to use to produce the desired result, and do so consciously? Thought is bound to produce some result. Negative thought will produce negative results, and positive thought positive results. This is the basis of all mental and spiritual science. We are just beginning to realize the dynamic energy of thought, and the greatest study we can engage in is a study of ourselves. We will find within ourselves that wonderful thing we are looking for: the power to create.

Scientists in laboratories are tearing elements to pieces, and where they used to peer through a lens of very low magnifying power, trying to search into the gross structure of the element, they now take infinitesimal particles of matter and subdivide them into intangible sparks, tiny bundles of electrical energy whirling at terrific speeds around one another according to intelligent and accurate law. We are just beginning to appreciate the nature of the physical universe, and through it we are beginning to deduce the nature of Mind and Spirit.

There is an intelligence behind all natural processes, and if we were to speak of the process of intelligence as being thought, then we can truly say that there is an Infinite God, Spirit, Supreme Intelligence, or any other name that conveys the idea of infinite personhood and limitless knowingness. The universe is really a thing of thought. This in no way denies its physical nature, but merely affirms that this physical nature is the manifestation of intelligence.

If God's world is a world of thought, then our world must also be a thing of thought. Of course we are not yet completely conscious of this, and therefore by the very power that we might produce freedom, we create bondage. How are we going to turn bondage into freedom other than by reversing the operation of the law that produces bondage? We must substitute an intelligent use of the law for an ignorant use. In this way we will learn to no longer destroy, but always to construct. There is a definite law of thought reversal in psychology and metaphysics, and a definite technique for using this law. This is what a spiritual mind practitioner does. It stands to reason that this law should be used consciously and definitely and for specific purposes. It is also self-evident that certain kinds of thoughts produce certain types of manifestation, and that by directly reversing negative thought and in its places substituting positive thought, we can automatically change an undesirable condition.

God Is Personal, Yet Impersonal

As we better understand the nature of God through studying God's activity in the universe, it is only one step further for us to arrive at a more accurate idea of what God's view of humankind must be. We have found that there is a governing directive act of intelligence in the universe, whirling the electrons in a rock, a piece of steel, the leg of an ant or the brain of a philosopher, all in accordance with mathematical law which never varies by so much as a fraction. We must learn how to use this power with its mathematical accuracy in our daily affairs, because this would be a divine government.

Of course we know that we cannot change the laws of nature. We merely use them. There is nothing supernatural in the universe. The universe must be methodical; it must be the exact operation of a supreme intelligence. Intelligence must be omniscient and the law immutable. Natural laws never deviate. What is more reasonable than to suppose that those who place themselves in accord with these laws will find comfort, while those whose actions run counter to them will experience discomfort? Any punishment for the infraction of natural law is not a personal response on the part of a displease deity, but is the logical, impersonal outcome of an ever-operative law of cause and effect.

It is really wonderful to realize this, since it will teach us that there is no sin except a mistake and no punishment except a consequence. This understanding also places the responsibility of human action on we ourselves, who are automatically punished when we misuse the law of our being. The triumph of this perception is that salvation is already and always at hand. The supreme good is always available. There is no personal anger on the part of God against those who jump into deep water before they have learned to swim, nor is there any anger on the part of the water that drowns them. Law is always impersonal.

It is interesting to realize that the negative result of plunging into water before one has learned how to keep afloat is a natural sequence of cause and effect, not the will of God as punishment, but the will of God as natural law and order. It is equally interesting to realize that the laws of thought operate in a like manner. Mentally and spiritually, we sink and swim according to the way in which we use these laws.

At this point, you might ask, "Just how do we use them?" The answer seems self-evident. We use the laws of thought when we think. And the law of Mind responds to us as we think. It naturally follows that thoughts of impoverishment will bring impoverishment, while thoughts of abundance will bring prosperity. To learn how to control thought is to learn how to control destiny. As Moses rightly said, "The word is very nigh unto thee, in thy mouth." The entire philosophy of Jesus is built on the laws of thought. Believe, and it will be done.

God's View of Humankind

From all we have learned about the inner harmonious perfection of the universe, we know that its nature is one of extreme beneficence when we cooperate with it. Hence we arrive at the conclusion that God's will for us is happiness and that happiness is achieved through adhering to certain laws. It stands to reason that we cannot achieve happiness for ourselves without wishing it for others, because this would be a house divided against itself. The laws of the universe are immutable, exact and just. This justice is not vengeance, but rather it is balance, equilibrium, true compensation.

How wonderful to realize that we can use such laws, and we are using them at all times whether or not we are conscious of the fact. We are neither forgotten people nor are we favorites of God. The question of success and failure remains where it belongs, in the mastery of ignorance, in the overcoming of superstition, fear and doubt, in the elimination of destructive methods and in the conscious reversal of thought processes that deny the eternal good.

This we must do consciously. Never forget that it is not enough to merely state a principle. Principles are stated in order that we may understand them. Yet, being stated, they must be used. You will never get anywhere by just saying the universe is governed by thought. That is the principle you have to demonstrate, and if you wish to demonstrate that good is supreme, you must learn how to enforce this principle by conscious cooperation with it. This is neither difficult to understand nor hard to do. It is a matter of choice. It requires no great powers of concentration or special necessity for deep meditation or contemplation. Learn to make it very simple and to build your thought processes and your imagination around the belief that good is supreme, realizing that this supreme good comes to you only as you first wish it for others.

No Limitation

It seems self-evident that limitation is not intended for us. The only limitation that life imposes on us is the necessity that we will comply with its laws. Universal Intelligence expresses through every material form through what we call simple things and in what we call complex things. We may set it down as a law of nature that the expression of Divine Intelligence is limited only by the capacity of the organism to express this intelligence. The Spirit itself knows no limitation. The physical universe exists in the mind of God as an idea before it takes on material form. Something does not come from nothing, and it is basic to this entire system of thought that we should understand that behind every physical form is an idea holding that form in place. You and I did not create the divine ideas, but we do use them, and in our use of them we cause them to take the form of our thought. Thus we attract or repel, build or destroy, increase or diminish.

In our journey toward self-discovery, we have climbed a long and difficult evolutionary pathway. We have met all sorts of obstacles and apparent obstructions, but as our understanding deepens, we realize that all of these apparent limitations are merely the way in which an immutable law is working. This does not mean that God has set personal handicaps for us to overcome. The Spirit never tempts us. The trials through which we pass are inherent in a universal law, but they are not insurmountable. We either run away from our troubles or master them. The interesting thing is that we master them as we understand that law itself is an impersonal force, neither for us nor against us, but always working with us. Thus, adaptation makes survival and advance possible.

Why shouldn't we learn to adapt ourselves to the laws of thought as we are already learning to adapt ourselves to the laws of physics? Thought is not only the most dynamic energy humankind has ever discovered, but it is the final creative principle we know anything about. When we will have learned to think the thoughts of God, we will have discovered the pathway to success, happiness and physical well-being. But having discovered the principle, we must consciously make use of it. The thing to do is to begin right now. Don't wait!

Law Cooperates with Us

The creative intelligence of the universe is always cooperative. It is always waiting to pour in new reserves of strength and wisdom as we show our willingness to cooperate with the law of our being. The higher levels of God-intelligence have always been there. Our evolution consists of awakening to them, and our progress consists in learning how these laws operate and in learning how to consciously cooperate with them. We catch the laws of nature, as it were, and individualize them for specific purposes. Thus we make them do our bidding. We must learn to harness the energy of Mind just as we do the energy of electricity. If you want to be successful, think success; if you wish to be happy, think happiness; if you want friends, become friendly. Do more than this. Declare that your word is the law in your experience. At once, you will find the law is the silent partner in the firm of God and Company, obeying your will.

Application for Today

Suppose you are faced with what seems an impossible situation, a business or health condition that seems hopeless. Realize that it is only hopeless from the angle from which you are now viewing it. There is always a way out. You should realize that the law is automatically reflecting your own thought about it. Therefore, you must learn to give vigorous denial to any voice that speaks of a hopeless state. Know that all the power in the universe waits for your command. Face the situation not in the whipped or whimpering attitude of those who depend only on their own human resources, but in the confident attitude of those who know that they are linked with a law, a power and a presence that will reflect back to them their own courageous attitude, magnifying their thought a million times.

Feel that this power is flowing in as freedom. It flows over and through the limiting circumstance and transmutes poverty into abundance, sickness into health, fear into faith. Also remember that the power was there before you recognized it. If you wish its flow to be one of happiness, you must provide a channel through which it may become the objective manifestation of your inner desire. It is impossible to demonstrate success while identifying yourself with failure. We never stand alone. "The angel of the Lord (law) encamps around about them that fear the Lord and delivers them." It is this universal power of law animated by love which dissolves our human problems. What mental imagery is sufficient to do this other than the mental imagery that conceives of God as being the only power there is? Our part is fearlessly to face any apparently difficult situation and, instead of seeing the difficulty, transmute all fear into the faith of one who really believes.

Our View of Ourselves

Our view of ourselves probably has been nearly opposite of what God's view of God's self must be like. Are we not always thinking of ourselves as sinful, wicked, sick, unhappy, defeated? The law, being impersonal, is always trying to make these thoughts come true in our experience. The secret of self-mastery lies in turning away from this negative view of oneself and accepting as a divine birthright that which the inner intuitive sense feels must be so. If God is for us, who can be against us?

We are free, but we do not know it. We live like servants instead of sovereigns. Occasionally, in moments of illumination, we see or sense our heritage of freedom. When we do this, we have caught the God view. We must not allow the old lifetime habit of fear to reassume dominance or the untrue, distorted pictures of negative belief to overlay the truth.

Sometimes our thought is a mixture of good and evil, and so we experience first one and then the other. Mind, or the creative principle that surrounds us, is then faced with the task of projecting not one clear picture, but two. And because these two pictures are in opposition to each other, they produce confusion. We must realize that one clear concept steadily held in mind *will* manifest itself. We have the privilege and we certainly have the power to determine which picture is to predominate, because success or failure in experience will be the result of these pictures of thought.

❦

Meditation

I know there is no power in the universe that is opposed to my good. There is no God who desires me to be sick or unhappy. I know that all things work together for good to those who love God. I recognize the truth of the statement "All's love, but all's law," and as I feel my unity with this love principle at the heart of things, my difficulties dissolve and disappear. The Creator's power flows through my experiences and recreates them in the eternal pattern of the divine perfection.

❦

Questions

1. Are disease and misery due to the displeasure of God?
2. Is punishment ever personal?

3. What is the important thing about God's view of humankind?
4. Are we intended to be limited?
5. How should one face a seemingly hopeless situation?

Answers

1. Disease and misery are not due to the displeasure of God, but are the consequences of our own mistakes.
2. No. Punishment is an impersonal consequence. The laws of the universe are causal and not vindictive.
3. The important thing about God's view of humankind is that we are intended for happiness, and we can achieve it when we learn how to use the impersonal power of law.
4. There is no cosmic intention of limitation for us. Limitation is primarily a result of a belief that the universal Intelligence is hampered in its expression through us.
5. One should face a seemingly hopeless situation by knowing that there must be a way out. We should recognize that the vast resources of Cosmic Intelligence are at our disposal, leading us to a solution of every situation however complex.

Spirit, the Actor; Mind, the Law; Creation, the Result

Children see a mechanical contraption, and their first reaction to it is one of interest in its action. They enjoy seeing it work, and that is the end of their interest, because their minds are as yet only at the stage where the practical, concrete, apparent movement is important. Later on, as their minds develop, they will pass on to the "why" and the "how" of its working, because then they will have reached the state where they recognize a relationship between cause and effect. This is because reason has dawned in their intellectual processes. It is not sufficient that they see action; they must go behind the action to discover, if possible, the logical reason for the activity.

Adults are similarly responsive to things they have never before experienced or seen. For example, we may have become attracted to the Science of Mind by some apparent "miracle of healing." It may have been a remarkable demonstration of supply seen in the life of a student of this Science or of the solution of a seemingly intricate problem. But whatever is was that first attracted our attention, it was some action or activity compelling enough to draw our attention. But that is as far as many people ever go. These are the child minds, which never go on to seek the reasons behind the phenomena that they have seen.

The growing mentality, always alert to learn and understand new truths, can never be satisfied with the mere objective observation of the phenomena of Mind. It just goes behind the outer to search the inner for the reasons. The child mind is satisfied to hear the watch tick; the growing mind must find out what makes it tick. This book was written for the growing mind. You would never have started reading unless you had been going deeper than the mere casual observer. This book therefore goes behind creation, past the effects that we see to the cause that produces them.

The Meaning of Creation

When we speak of creation, we should have a clear concept of what we mean. Creation really means giving form to a formless substance. The creative principle, which is God, is at the center of everything that lives. From our viewpoint, the creative power means an ever-present reality, and of course an ever-available one that is not only at the center of our being, but in which we are immersed. That is, it is in us and we are in it. We should not lose sight of the thought that the original and originating creative Mind around us is the same Mind that is in us. God is one, not two.

From this viewpoint, creation does not mean making something out of nothing. Rather, it means giving form to something that already exists. The energy, the substance and the intelligence of the universe have always existed and always will, but the operation of the laws of thought on this creative substance causes it forever to take new forms. Thus creation always goes on as an eternal activity of God.

God is personal to us because God is personified in us. God is operative through us because the creative process of thought is always going on within us, and some form of creation is always following in our individual experience. Thus each of us individualizes and personifies God. Mostly this has been done in ignorance, but we are learning now how to do it definitely, with conscious design. We are learning to make a miniature cosmos out of an apparent chaos, bringing heaven to earth, as it were. One of the most interesting things we will discover is that this is done not by compulsion but through imagination, using only enough will in the process to hold thought in one place long enough to permit a definite creation to take place

"God In," Not "God And"

Creation always means that God is giving form to an eternal sub-stance. God creates not by bringing something out of nothing, but by giving outer form to something formless that has always existed, being coexistent with Spirit from the beginning. This substance, which is both invisible and impalpable, must always have been in existence because the universe, Mind and Spirit are an indivisible unity. Thus when God creates, God creates only the form, which may be of any shape and substance to the material sense, but is nevertheless always the same primary material.

We never say God *and* us or God *and* anything, because it is God *in* us or God *in* anything that has form. Thus when we say that there is nothing except God, we understand what we mean, even though the outsider might argue that God is Spirit and the universe is mat-ter. We understand that God is *in* and *is* the thing that God creates.

It is an understanding of this that makes it possible for us to see why sickness and lack are not things in themselves. They are real enough as experience, but they are never real from the standpoint of ultimate reality. It is self-evident that the God-principle can be nei-ther sick nor limited. This enables us to understand that Spirit is the real actor, constantly putting itself into form. This will also enable us to see that when we recognize the God-principle in some person or situation, it will respond to us. The thing to remember is that we do not place the God-principle in things; we merely recognize that it is there. God Power is already in everything. We are saturated with it.

There is a difference between God Power and God Presence. God Presence means the Divine Being, the essence of our own divinity, the indwelling God, the Spirit within to whom Jesus prayed. God Power means the law of Mind working in us. God Presence is personal; God Power is merely a law of cause and effect. When we recognize the God Presence, then the God Power responds according to this recognition. We must never overlook this, because it is really the secret of our power to demonstrate or to bring greater good into our individual experience or into the experience of others. Instead of thinking of sickness, we must think of health, and we are able to think of health when we realize the God Presence as perfect. It is a realization of this God Presence as perfect that causes the God Power to respond as harmony rather than discord.

In order to do effective work, the realization of this God Presence and God Power must be more than theoretical; it must be specific. Always try to feel that at the very center of the person for whom you are praying, the client, there is a God Presence responding to you and a God Power corresponding to your mental states. In mental prayer treatment, when you use the word *action*, know that action takes place. When you use the word *peace*, know that because God is present as peace, then the law of Mind must produce a peaceful condition or situation.

Spirit is the only actor, and in a certain sense it is perfectly correct to say that God must be recognized if God is going to manifest God's self to us, because we will be like God when we see God as God is. When we are looking at our physical bodies, we should feel that we are looking at some part of the body of God. We should transpose all thoughts of sickness into thoughts of health. When we look at our business of activity, whatever it may be, we must see the principle of life animating it and declare that this animating principle and power is active in our affairs. This is not willpower, but awareness. This awareness must definitely be used if one expects to get results. It is like anything else in the universe; it exists merely as a potential until we make conscious use of it. In the Science of Mind, the conscious use that we make of power is brought about by consciously directing thought, making specific statements, etc.

Mind: The Infallible Law

Creation is accomplished though the working of a law that is as infallible as the law that runs through mathematics. If the law or numbers were to vary from day to day, so that six would be six today and eight tomorrow, there could be no certainty in life. Our whole civilization, indeed our very existence, is based on the certainty of the law of numbers. The saying "Figures don't lie" is not merely a clever saying. It is the statement of the fact that a universe is possible.

Many people who accept the infallibility of the law that runs through numbers have not yet seen the infallibility of creative law. This law, set in motion by Spirit through the word of God, moves immutably in the direction pointed out by the Word. "In the beginning was the Word, and the Word was with God and the Word was God. Without God was not anything made that was made." The Word represents the ability of Spirit to declare itself into form.

This whole action of Spirit must be within itself upon the law, which also must be within itself to mold the universal stuff or substance, which is also within itself. Thus we have God working upon God's self to spin out from God's self that which we call material substance. This action of the Spirit on itself is what is meant by the Divine Trinity—the Creator, or the Creative Spirit; the Child, or that which is created; and the Holy Spirit, or the law of Mind in action.

We should never doubt the ability of Mind to bring to pass that which our word decrees in it. To doubt the power of our word would be to automatically shut ourselves off from this power. This is the meaning of the saying "They could not enter in because of their unbelief and because they limited the Holy One of Israel." What we should do is consciously align ourselves with the power, believe in it, become convinced that it is true, and have implicit faith and confidence in its action for us. Since we are individuals with self-choice, we should feel that we have a right to decide what we wish to experience, always feeling that our desires are molded by Divine Intelligence.

We should never desire anything that could hurt or limit anyone or do any harm whatsoever. It is reasonable to assume that when our desires are in harmony with the creative principle, we should feel free to let loose the reins of our imagination and expect to receive all the good that we can think of. If we think the power of God is almighty, or if we wish to state the proposition another way and say that the law of Mind is immutable, then we will readily see that limitation is not inherent in the law. Our limitation is the way we have used a law that, of itself, is without limit. In a certain sense, we create bondage out of freedom. But we never destroy freedom and we really never create bondage. Our bondage is merely a limited concept of freedom.

Emergent Evolution

When we make a demand on the creative principle, the answer to that demand emerges out of this principle. There is a doctrine in philosophy that states that whenever intelligence makes a demand on itself, it answers its own demand out of its own nature. Whenever one has a desire to create that which is constructive, this desire is actually inspired by the indwelling Spirit that seeks expression through everything. The Spirit does not implant this desire in order to mock us but to fulfill its own nature. Thus Jesus said, "I am come that they might have life and that they might have it more abundantly."

Both the demand that Spirit makes on us and the demand that we make on Spirit should be considered spiritual in their natures. Even that which seems to be material, such as the desire for physical health or the proper amount of money, is God seeking self-expression. When we spiritualize our desires, we are aligning them with the nature of God, of harmony, and wherever we have a desire that is in line with harmony and accept its fulfillment, we will be using the creative law in a constructive and effective way.

To be certain of definite results, the proper way to use this law is to follow the method that Jesus laid down, because no better method has ever been developed. He very definitely said that when we pray for things, we should *believe* that we *already have* them, even before we see them. This seems like a contradiction until one understands the nature of the law involved. The law works on idea. It works on our thought, our belief, our imagination, and therefore in the final analysis it works on our *acceptance.*

Why is it that often when we try to believe some good is ours, it is so difficult to actually be convinced that this good is manifesting in our experience? What is it that arises within us to slay our thought of abundance, of health and happiness? Something really does seem to arise from within our consciousness to deny our good. This is the enemy that we must destroy. But what is it other than thought arising out of the deep subconscious well of our inner mind? The whole human race has believed in tragedy for so long that this suggestion of race belief arises within each one of us. We must detect it and deny its power, always affirming in its place the Divine Presence. This is the way to use the law. Do so definitely. Never be chaotic in your use of it. Always be specific.

If you want money, ask for money. If you want friends, ask for friends. But when you ask, *believe* that you have that for which you are asking.

Harmony in Desire

We said that desire is a promise of fulfillment. This must be qualified, however, by the statement that the desire must be in line with the nature of the universe. If that desire hurts another by its fulfillment or takes away from those that which rightfully belongs to them, then it is clearly not in accord with the nature of the universe. It is a fundamental principle of our philosophy that *nothing in the universe wishes to do us harm.* Since all people are expressions of God, indwelt by God, then it logically follows that the one who wishes to harm another would be making God wish to harm God's self. Jesus presented this truth when he said that if he, by Beelzebub, cast out devils, then the house of truth was divided against itself.

When we each come to see and to know that nothing in the universe carries harm for us, we will understand why we say that "when God makes a demand on God's self, God answers that demand out of God's own nature." We admit that this is a far cry from the understanding of the average person who is prey to one thousand and one diseases, but it is entirely possible to those whose concept of the essential unity of the universe is a vital, living one, felt through and through.

Guidance through Law

Suppose there is a desire for right action or for the right movement when one comes to a fork in the road. We recognize that this desire is made by Spirit within us and that this demand is made by Spirit upon itself. Therefore, we rest quietly in the inner assurance that Spirit already knows the right answer and that Mind is already moving in the right direction. The right answer or right action is immediately created in Divine Mind and will be projected through our consciousness when we become entirely relaxed, expecting the law to move us in the right direction.

The trouble is that the untutored become panicky when a crisis comes. They rush to and fro, asking directions from anyone who is willing to give advice. They forget that there exists *within themselves* the answer to every question and the solution of every problem; that Spirit makes the demand and will answer that demand from within when they allow themselves to wait for the mental storm to die down. "Be still, and know" is the secret of guidance, as it is for every problem of life. A perturbed mind can never get the correct answer; a stilled person always can, because the answer comes from the God within.

Desires in Tune with the Infinite

We all wish to be well and happy and to enjoy healthy business and financial conditions. These desires are all in line with the universe, bringing harm to no one nor taking away from anyone that which rightfully belongs to them. We know that there is enough and to spare for all and that each one of us attracts our own good. The more we open our consciousness to the harmonious stillness and to the God within, the more surely we will begin to manifest that which was there all the time awaiting the action of Spirit, *through the law*, to give it form.

In opening our consciousness to this infinite presence within us, we are still subject to the exact laws of cause and effect. The universe is a cosmos and not a chaos. The most exalted spiritual faith is still in line with law, and we should be very glad that this is true, otherwise there would be nothing on which we might depend with absolute certainty.

It is not enough for us merely to know that there is enough good for all. We must follow this right knowing by declaring that this infinite good, which is God, is manifesting in our personal experience or in the experience of the one for whom we are working today. We may set it down as axiomatic in this Science that nothing can come out of a mental treatment unless we first put it in. This does not mean we put anything into the universe itself. We actually take everything out of it. We never create power; we *use* power. But simply because we do use power and do take something out of the universe, it seems logical to assume that we will take out of it only what we *believe* we will have to furnish our own thought pattern.

We might state the proposition another way and say that even God cannot give us what we refuse to accept. Therefore, we should create a mental picture of ourselves as daily receiving the good we desire. We should go further than this and train ourselves to expect more good. We should train the mind to visualize the perfect rather than the imperfect, and always there should be a sense of enthusiastic joy.

Be consciously specific in every treatment you give, and learn to believe that when you have made a statement, it is actually going to come true. As an example, take this simple thought. Suppose you are treating yourself for friendship and use a statement similar to this: "I am surrounded by loving friends. Everywhere I go, I meet people who enjoy my company." If you do make such a statement, you should believe that statement is actually an enforcement of a divine law. The statement focuses your belief and directs the power of your faith to a definite purpose. If law governs everything, then it governs the movement of thought. This is what we mean when we say that nothing can come out of a treatment unless we first put it in.

❧

Mediation

Today I recognize my unity with God, the indwelling presence. I know that since I am some expression of the Divine Being, every other person in the world must likewise be such an expression, and so I am really one with everybody. It follows then that in trying to harm another, I am actually injuring myself. I therefore refuse to consider doing anyone harm and deliberately work to bring good to all, knowing that the good of another is my good, just as the hurt of another is my hurt.

Since I am one with God and one with all humankind, there is no reason for loneliness or friendlessness. I live in a friendly universe, and I attract into my environment all those who will do me good and whom I can help. Thus my life is filled with happiness, and I rejoice and am glad.

❧

Questions

1. Is creation ever finished?
2. Why do we say "God in" and not "God and"?

3. What do we mean by God Presence and God Power?
4. What definite principle of prayer did Jesus state?
5. How can we tell what we have a right to ask for in prayer?

Answers

1. Any individual creative series becomes completed, but new series are constantly beginning because creation is an eternal activity of God.

2. We say "God in" and not "God and" because we recognize that there is no separation between God and the universe. God is in this creation, but not absorbed by it.

3. God Presence means the indwelling God, the Creator Almighty, the Spirit within. God Power is the law of Mind, or God working in the universe. The one is personal; the other impersonal.

4. Jesus stated a law of believing faith. When we ask for a thing, we must believe that we already have it. The subjective embodiment of the idea must precede any desired effect.

5. We can ask for and expect anything, provided only that what we desire will bring no harm either to ourselves or anyone else.

The Absolute and the Relative

One of the first things a person inquiring into this system of thought comes up against is the teaching that, spiritually, humankind is the image and likeness of God. Such a statement seems contrary to the facts of human experience, because humankind seems to be anything but God's image. People are often cruel, bitter, disappointed and defeated. Those beginning a study of this system of thought are told that income is not a thing in itself, yet at the same time they may be confronted with their inability to meet necessary expenses. They have been told that, as an expression of Spirit, their body is a spiritual manifestation composed of perfect ideas. Yet even as they listen to such statements, they may be suffering pain of physical distress. These apparent contradictions often make the beginner in this Science wonder whether people interested in metaphysics are not slightly "touched in the head."

These difficulties, however, will disappear when one realizes that all such statements are made about the spiritual person and that if the spiritual person was not perfect, if we were not composed of divine ideas harmoniously adjusted to each other, then the universe would be a house divided against itself. As a matter of fact, we never deny that people are sick or that they suffer and have pain or that they are poor or limited in experience. What we affirm is that there is an absolute at the center of everything. This absolute in no way contradicts the relative. We affirm that God is perfect, that the spiritual person is perfect, that we are surrounded by spiritual substance that responds to thought impulses, and that there is an immutable law governing everything

We affirm a limitless universe, but in so doing we are not denying what appears to be a limited experience. We are merely affirming that our limited experience is a result of our limited use of this absolute universe. We are called on to imagine a universe that is so absolutely without limitation that nothing can limit it. We are also called on to imagine an individualized center of consciousness, which is humankind, having such complete freedom in this universe that even this freedom may be used in the form of bondage.

Here is a paradox. Is this bondage real or an illusion? Since God's world cannot be a world of illusion, it follows that bondage is not exactly an illusion. It is merely a limited way of using something that, of itself, is without limit. Is the infinite energy of electricity limited or bound because we use it to run an egg-beater? Of course the answer is "No!" Well, then, is the Creative Mind limited or bound because we use it to create unhappiness? Of course not. We could just as well use it for some other purpose.

One thing everyone studying this Science must be sure to understand is that the universe is a unity. There are not two powers opposed to each other, but one power that is used in different ways. This power is absolute; our way of using it is relative.

Definition of the Absolute

The absolute may be defined as the unconditioned; that which nothing can limit; that which forever transcends any conceivable limitation or determination; unconditioned perfection, self-sufficient and self-existent. It is often used as a synonym for God. Truth is absolute and remains unaffected by the opinions, desires or beliefs of the individual.

From the beginning, the Infinite has always existed in a total and unchangeable state of perfection. There has never been for a single fleeting moment one slightest tinge of doubt in the Mind of God. God does not and can not know what doubt is, because God knows only truth. Since truth cannot be divided, there is no part of it that can be lacking in the Mind of God. God knows only God's self, because there is nothing else in the universe. Therefore, it would be impossible for God to know anything less than continuous perfection.

God could not possibly know or experience limitation. If God could know evil, God could experience it, and this is unthinkable. God could never know anything less than peace, perfect peace. The Mind of God has never been ruffled by the slightest wind of turmoil.

God has never been able to see anything less than absolute beauty. There could be no distortion of form, no unbalance in the Mind of God, because it is impossible for God to know anything less than God's self. Distorted form is an impossibility to God.

God has never had, nor could have, any desire that God was unable to fulfill. Therefore, limitation at any point of God's being is unthinkable. Anything that God sees, God becomes. Any desire that God has comes into being in the same matchless perfection that God is in God's nature.

In the last analysis, truth is merely the statement of what God is in God's self. Therefore when we speak the truth, we declare the being of God in human words. Truth is not a set of rules or beliefs, except as they portray the absolute God.

Definition of the Relative

Since the absolute is first cause, it is also continuing cause. The relative is an effect of the absolute, which is its cause. Time, space, outline, form, change, movement, action and reaction, manifested creation, all are relative. This does not mean that they are unreal. Far from it! The relative is not apart from, but exists within the absolute. *It is not a thing in itself, but only that which functions within the absolute and depends on it.*

The relative could be defined as "existing only as an object of or in relation to a thinking mind." And here is where we have such wide variations in the relative. Some people have brought their understanding to a point at which it, to a remarkable degree, approximates the absolute, while others have varying degrees of cloudiness in the conceptions they entertain. Jesus referred to this when he said, "According to your faith, be it unto you." He knew that not all people had risen in consciousness to a point of faith from which they could view God and the universe as a perfect unity. He also knew that we could demonstrate in our experience only that which we were able to embody mentally through the power of faith.

The mere fact that there are such different degrees of relativity is an indication that the absolute exists as the perfect idea. In fact, *the mere existence of the relative universe is a guarantee that behind it there must be an absolute in which this relative universe exists.* We know of the existence of the real hidden cause through that which we can see and touch, the relative or objective world.

Practical Application

There is no particular value in going into these abstract discussions unless we draw practical conclusions from them. What we wish to be certain of is that our own world is absolute and unconditioned. We desire a firm foundation on which to build our practice of the Science of Mind, making it workable and practical in our everyday lives.

It is certain that the absolute cannot be changed. It is also certain that we cannot contract the absolute. It is equally certain that we can expand the relative. That is, while we cannot change the nature of God—nor indeed can we change our own natures—we can expand our experience in the divine nature. Knowledge alone gives power. When Jesus said there is a truth that we can know which will produce freedom, he must have been referring to the possibility of our having knowledge of our divine nature, which knowledge by the very fact of understanding it and using it must automatically produce freedom. It is evident that Jesus perceived the absoluteness of reality. He knew that the word of God is in and operating through humankind. Therefore, he made practical application of the spiritual knowledge. He plainly taught that we can expand our human horizons by realizing the divinity within us, which has no horizon, but which at the same time is always creating experiences.

Most of our fears, if not all of them, are the result of imperfect knowing, whether these fears take the form of pain, sickness, poverty or perhaps even death. All negative experience is a result of a belief that there is something other than life, or that life withholds pleasure, peace or success from us. From the standpoint of spiritual reality, this belief is always false. God, or life, does not withhold anything from us. False belief is healed by knowing the truth, which is that we live within the absolute, that we are capable of infinite expansion, and that our true nature is to be perfect even as the Spirit must be perfect.

The Spirit has never withheld good from us, but ignorance of the true law of supply has caused us to have fear. "They could not enter in because of their unbelief and because they *limited* the Holy One." As we stop limiting God, the God within us, we expand the relative. All things are already given unto us, but *we ourselves must do the taking.* The gift of heaven is forever made. The receiving of this gift is an external process of forever expanding the finite. The destiny of humankind is an eternal expansion. We come from God, are in and forever will remain in and one with God.

How We Embody Ideas

We embody an idea by giving our complete attention to it. This is carried on in Mind quite automatically. We select the idea, and Mind projects it into form. Thus we attract to ourselves our objective likeness of this embodiment. In other words, the thought becomes a thing. The mental state takes on form, color and temporary reality. Outwardly, we experience the states of our consciousness. But since an apparent outer is merely the reflection of an inner which is its cause, we need first to start with the simple proposition of the creative power of thought and, from this inner recognition, know that circumstances are formed and held in place through the action of the law of thought.

The relationship between the individual mind and the universal Mind is one of reflection. What we image for ourselves, it images for us. The law is that Mind images back for us the destructive as well as the constructive things that we first mentally image, just as a mirror will reflect a ghastly face or one of beauty. It follows, therefore, that the very law of freedom that enables us to rise to the heights may operate as a law of limitation to bind us in chains. The blame for the consequence lies only in ourselves. Change the face in the mirror, and the reflection immediately changes.

By its very nature, the Divine wills freedom for us. However, since we are real individuals having creative thoughts, the law, which is impersonal, makes for death as well as life, bondage as well as freedom, sickness as well as health, poverty as well as plenty. In other words, "It's up to you."

We Rule through Obedience

We are intended to rule, but we rule as we learn obedience to this power that is over us. As we live in obedience to this power, we will be able to consciously direct the lesser conditions that are around us. In ancient symbolism, Adam was permitted to name all creation because humankind was supposed to exercise an authority over all that is below it. We have done this to a remarkable degree in the word of animal life and in the physical universe, but we have failed too often in controlling our immediate environment. This we must learn, because it is included in our gift of power.

Physically, we are weaker than the lion, tiger and elephant. Yet through our recognition of our potentialities, we have subdued them. They will never wipe humankind off the face of the earth, but we may do this to them. We have conquered the elements and have made the earth from which we sprang yield to our will and bring forth the particular crops that we desire.

Nowadays there is a growing recognition of the fact that other details of our environment are likewise under our direct control. Thus we are learning to subdue sickness through a correct use of the power of Mind. We are learning that it is not "ordained" for us to go through life denied the good things that add to our comfort. We are learning that we can build a business, add to our income, increase our talents and make a complete change in our manner of living as we come to understand this law of reflection that gives back to us that which we give to it.

Experiences Do Not Change Facts

You can either sit in the shade or move into the sunshine. Sitting in the shade, you may tell yourself that there is no sunshine, but the fact is that the sun shines continuously, and the only sunlessness is the darkness within your own mentality. If you believe in suffering, you will suffer. That suffering will be real, not fancied, but the foundation on which the suffering is built is an unreal foundation. Moreover, it is unnecessary. When you approach life from the standpoint of truth, life will respond to you in the very same manner.

Life is a blackboard before which we stand and write the words that govern us. We hold both chalk and the eraser in our hands. The blackboard allows us to use either chalk or eraser on it, according to our power of will or choice. If we have made scrawling, incorrect marks on the blackboard, we need not condemn ourselves, nor need we go through life bemoaning their presence. We do not have to go through life paying for the mistakes of yesterday. The important thing is that the hand that holds the eraser must do the erasing.

Spirit can never be antagonistic toward us. It is always flowing through us into the kind of expression we allow it to have. The self-expression of God is the self-expression of humankind, because the two are one.

We must learn to affirm the truth of Being in the face of all contrary experience. Even when our outer experience cries loudly to the contrary, we must continue to know and to affirm that we are each a center of God-consciousness, heirs to all the perfection that the Infinite is. This very affirmation heals because it is a statement of the truth that makes wholeness.

There is a vast difference between realizing that these things are so and actually demonstrating them. Unfortunately we too frequently think that the statement of the principle demonstrates the activity of its law, but such is not the case. It is not enough in this Science to state merely that God is all there is; this statement was true before you said it. You must finish this statement by saying, "… because there is one Infinite Mind. That Mind is my mind now, and because that Mind is my mind right now, it is guiding me into right decisions and right action." This is the principle of divine guidance. It is not enough merely to say there is abundance in the universe; we must also add, "This abundance is now manifest as my supply." If we fail to do this, we will fail to connect the absolute with the relative. We will be making correct statements of natural principles, but we will not be using the law that promotes our individual well-being.

Too much cannot be said in favor of beginning at once to practice this Science. It is useless to merely study it. It is something that must be used and used consciously and with definite intention. When you give a mental prayer treatment, you put into that treatment everything you wish to have happen. That is, you say in words what you want to take place, whether it is for yourself or for someone else. After having used any words that will convey such meaning to your own mind, state, "This is the law unto this thing or this person." In this way you are correctly observing the letter of the law. Your next step is to enter a state of realization or enter into your good, into the atmosphere of it, always feeling that it is so. This adds the Spirit to the letter of the law and makes perfect the whole process.

∽

Meditation

I know that I am made spiritually in the image and likeness of God. My conscious thought is a reflection of the self-conscious Spirit of the universe. The law of my being is the immutable law of God. My body is the expression of the divine ideal of humankind. I know that I am in essence perfect and entire, wanting in nothing. Any bondage of body or circumstances that I express is not a condition imposed on me by a vindictive deity. My bondage is the result of my freedom of thought and my choice of limitation. Today I deliberately choose to let the perfect image and likeness of God shine through me, and I erase from my consciousness all limiting thought. Thus I know that my experience in this body of flesh and in the body of my circumstances reflects the perfect spiritual person, the undefiled creation of the good and unlimited God.

∽

Questions

1. In the Science of Mind philosophy, do we ever deny sickness or pain?
2. Do we deny limitation?
3. Does God ever doubt God's own ability to act?
4. How do we embody an idea?
5. Should we feel that we ought to go through life denying ourselves the good things of life?

Answers

1. We don't deny the experience of sickness or pain, but we affirm that behind the experience is a perfect spiritual person who has never been sick or suffered.

2. We do not deny limitation in experience. We affirm that the limited experience is the result of our use of the law. We put limitation into the limitless and will draw out limitation as experience as long as we continue to do this.

3. God cannot know doubt, because that would be belief of limitation, and the Absolute could not know limitation.

4. We embody an idea by giving our complete attention to it. As a result of this embodiment, we attract into our experience the objective correspondent of the idea thus embodied.

5. We should learn that we can build our business, add to our income and live comfortably and graciously through the correct use of the power of Mind. There is no deity who desires to deprive us of the right enjoyment of life.

Law and Personality

❧

It seems scarcely necessary to say that there is a deep, active spirit of inquiry abroad in the word today. People everywhere are searching for truth, perhaps as never before in the history of humankind. The remarkable feature of this search, however, is that not only the common person, but the scientist in laboratory is probing deep into the universe trying to find the source of our being.

There is definitely growing recognition of the fact that the universe shows activity on two different planes or in two different directions. We are coming to recognize that there are forces that operate strictly and all the time according to fixed laws and apparently without any volition on their part. At the same time, it is observed that the highest force of all, the force of thought, is a personal, volitional form of energy. The two have seemed to be contradictory to one another, and consequently we are confronted with two groups of thinkers: those who maintain that humankind is fixed in a treadmill of life in which we are part of and subject to the blind working of unchangeable law and have very little, if anything, to say about the matter; and those on the other hand who ignore or depreciate the working of law and who consequently struggle along through life by a process of "trial and error." It is possible to reconcile these two apparently conflicting views, because when seen in their true relation to one another, they will be found to be complementary, not antagonistic.

Unquestionably, thought is power, and it operates by law. It is not a vague, unpredictable influence floating around in the universe. Properly understood, thought is subject to as exact laws as those of chemistry or any other physical science. But at the same time, *the individual has the fullest freedom.*

We Live and We Are Thinkers

There are two observable facts of which we can be certain. The first is that we live. It is impossible for sane people to doubt the reality of their own experience. The second fact is that there is a universe around us. We experience this universe every time we bump our heads on something.

The next logical question would be, then, what is it in us that knows these two facts? It certainly is not the flesh, because we can continue to think even with our legs cut off. But those legs cannot think apart from us. Therefore, there must be something in us that is able to receive and interpret impressions from the universe, to conceive ideas, to reason concerning life and to determine which activities will follow which conclusions. *That "something" is the real "I" myself.*

It is equally observable that the brain does not do the thinking, because the brain removed from the body has no power to think. The brain is the material organ through which the thinker thinks. We each, in our true inner selfhood, are the thinker.

Natural Forces Do Not Think

It is also observable that the forces of nature do not think. Our whole system of science is based on this factual observation. The forces of steam, gravitation, electricity and every other natural force operate strictly under laws. If there were no fixed laws by which they operated, there could be no science, because the shifting bases would render it impossible to rely on things always being in the same place and working in the same way. Neither they nor we have any power to alter to the slightest degree those laws under which they act.

We have, therefore, two manifestations of activity: the movement of thought, which is based on the consciousness and will of humankind; and the movement of natural, universal energy based on an exact mathematical sequence of cause and effect. When we are able to reconcile these two modes of action, we can understand why life is what it is, and better still, we can make life what we wish it to be. So we seek to learn the nature of matter and that of Mind.

The Nature of Matter

Every material object in the universe is composed of certain units called *elements*. Phosphorus, sodium and uranium are elements, and there are over ninety more of them already known. The elements hydrogen and oxygen when combined according to a certain chemical formula become water. All substances are different because of the various groupings of the elements of which they are composed, and all matter is composed of elements. The physical person is composed of some, perhaps all, of the elements of which the earth is made, except in our bodies they are in different combinations and proportions.

Finer Subdivisions of Matter

An observable lump of matter is proportionately large compared to the tiny particles of which it is composed. If the matter were to be broken down, it would resolve itself into atoms. Going further, an atom is huge compared with the particles of which it is composed.

These infinitesimal particles of which atoms are composed are called, in general, electrons, although there are distinctive names for various kinds of electrons.

To illustrate, if we were to crush rock down to its finest possible powder, so fine you could not detect it between your teeth, that tiny dust would contain certain elements. If we could separate these elements further, they would break down into atoms and ultimately into tangible particles called electrons.

The atom is made up like a miniature solar system. There is a "nuclear sun" at its center with a chain or circle of electrons whirling at almost unbelievable speeds around it. An idea of the sizes and distances involved in a particle of matter may be gained by considering the fact pointed out by physicists that if a drop of water were as large as the earth, a chemical atom would comparatively be as large as a baseball. If we could think of this atom as being as large as the Empire State Building, its electrons would be as small as the heads of pins. Furthermore, in proportion to the size of the electrons, the distance at which they travel around the nucleus is as great as the distance at which the earth travels around our sun, approximately 93,000,000 miles.

If this is not too staggering for us to think of, it might be well to go on and ask, "What are electrons made of?"

Electrons are infinitesimal particles of electricity, hence their name. The central sun is positively charged; the revolving particles are negatively charged. Electricity is therefore the most highly attenuated form of matter. It is also a form of energy. It might be said that these electrons, the ultimate basis of matter, are energy condensed down to its *most* tangible form, and that they are at the same time formed matter in its *least* tangible form. In other words, in the electron, we see energy changing into matter. So when we say in treating the sick, "This person's body is spiritual substance," we have scientific support for the statement.

All Matter Is One Substance

Science has thus shown that every kind of atom is composed of these particles. Thus there must be one original substance present everywhere in the universe which occupies all space. The nature of the particular atom or particular object is determined by the number of its particles, their distance from the central nuclear sun, and their rate of rotation around the sun. Truly, the entire universe is one, just as all Mind is one. But let us leave substance for a time and go on to see what we can learn about the Thinker behind all substance.

The Nature of the Thinker

We have found that all matter is one and that all Mind is one. The mind with which we think is the Mind that governs these tiny planetary systems that comprise matter. We saw earlier that matter has no power to move itself, but must be acted on by a force outside of itself. The force that moves the body is the power of thought, and the intelligence that is behind thought is the intelligence that runs the universe. Matter in itself possesses no power of thought or of independent action, but it is so saturated with thought that it moves as the thought moves.

This Thinker is always thinking perfectly, but the mind-stuff or intelligence or thought must flow through the mental states of humankind. The student might well ask at this point, "What is the difference between Mind and mental states?" There is a real difference, and one that should be held clearly by the student. Mental states are the molds that hold this universal "thought-stuff" in varying forms. We might liken it to the vast surrounding atmosphere that we force into balloons of varying sizes, shapes and colors. It is still the same atmosphere, but through our power of selection we can force it into any shaped balloon we wish. We can allow the perfect thought of perfect intelligence to flow into a twisted, distorted mental state, and by the same law that would manifest perfection as a perfect mental state, it will manifest distortion as a distorted mental state.

Matter Reflects Mental States

We can readily understand why it is that material forms must be manifestations of mental states. They are Mind in visible form. The physical universe around us was not, of course, created by our individual thought. It is created by the thought of God, or the Universal Thinker, but since the Mind of God is also the mind of humankind, or the mind *in* humankind, it follows that our use of this Mind individualizes its creative power in a personal way. One's body, business or material possessions are spiritual substance enclosed in a form that we give them.

Since the whole human race has believed in limitation throughout the ages, it follows that the limitation created by the race thought operates through all of us to a large degree. Whether we choose to call this race thought the human mind, the carnal mind, the collective unconscious or race suggestion makes no difference. It is probable that the sum total of human thought binds most of us until we consciously free ourselves by breaking down this human thought, by seeing through it, by knowing it for exactly what it is.

Hell is real enough to those who believe in it, but when we transpose the thought of hell for a contemplation of heaven, its supposed flames are at once extinguished. Lack and limitation are real enough in our experience, but if we can push our thought away from them and visualize a greater abundance, having faith that it will appear, then we will discover that the race thought about limitation merely holds circumstances in a certain limited form. The power that we use in doing this is the same power that creates everything, and since it has no limitation of itself and could have none, the only limitation that it has for us is the one we give to it.

This knowledge is a source of great encouragement, because when we see it, we know that "what thought has done, thought can undo." We have come to the place where we are able to reconcile these two apparently irreconcilable ideas—that of a world of immutable law, and that of a free personality. Stretching before us, way off into a limitless universe, is absolute perfection. We live in a universe pervaded by perfect intelligence and operated through a perfect law. At the same time, we possess free will to choose to set our thought, our mental states, in tune with the infinite perfection, knowing that the law will cement these concepts in our body and our environment. If there is any mystery of life, we can know that it is a "sweet mystery," and we can be glad that we have found it.

To Change the Mental States

We can always change our dominant mental states. Just as we could thrust a pin into our ugly balloons and release their enclosed air to the great surrounding air, so we can thrust the pin of our choice into any undesirable thought form. But in doing this, we must separate our action from our emotional reactions. We must know that will is in the field of Spirit and that the emotional states are in the realm of subjectivity. The "feelings" are the result of a lifetime of living in the feelings. They are habitual, and they clamor for control.

It is the individual's place to separate these feelings into their proper fields, recognize them for what they really are and proceed to assert the dominance of Spirit. We should recognize that our "feeling" life is subjective. Being subjective, it is under the direction of our conscious Spirit life. If we remember that the subjective is largely habitual and that when it seeks to flow back into the old thought form, it is because it has flowed in that direction unchecked for so long as to have become habitual, we will then approach our problem with eyes open to the truth.

By the subjective being largely habitual is meant that our thought patterns tend to perpetuate themselves unless or until they are changed. The happy thing to remember is that these thought patterns are always subjective, always in the subconscious part of thought. And since the subjective or subconscious can be changed by the conscious intention, these old thought patterns may be brought to the surface and their power to perpetuate themselves dissolved by the very act of mentally knowing that they no longer have any power.

It is necessary that you understand this, and it may be a help to you to know that all psycho-analytical processes are conducted on the principle that thought patterns can be brought to the surface and that, by being consciously known, their negative power becomes dissipated. In psychology, this is called catharsis and conversion. A similar process takes place in our own work as we seek to realize that lack, limitation, fear, doubt, sickness and pain could not be intended by the Divine Will. They are merely the misuse of our good. We must convert our old thought patterns into new and better ones.

This is the purpose of meditation, contemplation and spiritual mind treatment. The Science of Mind is very definite. It starts out with the assumption that there is a Mind principle around and within everyone and that this Mind principle creatively responds to thought. Hence, no matter what its response may have been previous to now, by changing the patterns of thought, we can change not its nature but the way in which it responds to us. In this process we are not fighting the devil or evil, nor are we contending against any form of bondage or limitation whatsoever. We are merely expanding the consciousness, and we should do so intentionally.

❧

Meditation

I know that God is, and that God is the totality of all existence. I know that in Spirit I live and move and have my being, and that I am therefore in essence Spirit. Since I am Spirit and therefore part of the infinite whole, this power inheres in me. When I speak my word consciously directing it to a definite purpose, it carries with it the power of God. It cannot return to me void, but it does run and prosper in the thing whereunto

I send it, because my word and the word of God is one word. I therefore speak my word with confidence and conviction, and in quietness await the resultant manifestation of my desire.

⌒∕☺

Questions

1. Does the brain think?
2. In what way does physical science help in the belief that there is only substance?
3. What is the ultimate power in the universe?
4. What are material forms?
5. How can we change our circumstances?

Answers

1. In this philosophy, we believe and teach that the brain does not think, but is the physical instrument through which Mind operates on this plane.
2. Physical science reduces matter to energy and number, suggesting that it is made up of one substance that takes different forms in correspondence to the number of units of that substance in a single atom together with the rate of motion of the electricity in the atom.
3. The ultimate power in the universe is thought.
4. Material forms are mental states in visible form.
5. We can change our circumstances by changing our dominant mental states.

THE LAW OF ATTRACTION

✑

We are always either attracting or repelling. It is impossible to escape this immutable law of cause and effect that governs everything. We are either drawing people to us or repelling them. Our thought is creating happy or unhappy experiences, sickness or health. If we are engaged in business, our thought decides whether or not our business is going to be successful, whether it will expand or contract. How necessary it becomes, then, for us to be independent in our thoughts. This is why Jesus once told his followers to judge not according to appearances.

We are always attracting either the love of others or their criticism. We are drawing assistance and cooperation into the orbit of our personal experience or we are creating frustrations and disappointments. This is because we are always thinking. Mind is the most active thing in the universe. It works ceaselessly fashioning thoughts into things. Everything we think goes into the grist-mill of Mind to come forth in our experiences.

We have reached a very happy place indeed and a desirable stage in our growth if we have come to the place where we no longer give expression to negative ideas. Always we should go on to higher levels, always we should be seeking to purify our thought processes. It must have been this idea that led the deep thinker of antiquity to say, "Let the words of my mouth and the meditations of my heart be acceptable in thy sight, oh Lord!" It is the hidden thought and belief that holds the outer form to the continuous activity of the creative Mind that surrounds us at all times.

Beliefs Produce Results

Most certainly Jesus laid down the fundamental law of mental life when he told us it is done unto us as we believe. How necessary it becomes, then, that we lay a solid foundation for our belief. Just what are we going to believe in? This is really what matters. Do we believe that the universe is for us or against us? Naturally our beliefs are personal, and we all hold individual thoughts about God and the universe. This is as it should be, but there are certain dominant beliefs that we should entertain and certain fundamental truths that we should all come clearly to see if we hope to make the most effective use of the Science of Mind. Surely we should come to believe that the universe is well disposed toward us, that God is love, that happiness is our divine birthright and that abundance belongs to everyone. Certainly we should believe that the normal state is to be physically well and, while we are in this world, financially secure.

It is certain that our fundamental beliefs color all of our experiences whether we are consciously thinking of them or not. Subconsciously, our beliefs are always working. It is not at all difficult to decide to change our conscious belief. It is easy enough to decide just what we desire, but if we are going to make this practical and effective, we must stay with our beliefs until they become a part of us. Belief must be based on conviction, or we will only be making believe that we believe. This would be to practice self-deception. We must find good and adequate reasons for believing, and then we must stay with them.

God in God's Universe

We know that the physical universe could not have created itself, because one of the major properties of matter is inertia. The physical universe of itself possesses no power of motion. It must always be moved and acted on by some force that is non-material, and the only non-material force is Intelligence. Since the physical universe antedates humankind by millions of years, we may be certain that our thought did not create it. It follows that the universe is a living presence. The simplest creature and the tiniest particle of matter are alive with the presence of God. In this living presence, which is the creative Spirit of the universe, we live and move and have our being, not as separated from the universe of Spirit, but as some part of it. We are each an individualized center of God consciousness, and each individual is a unique center. No two individuals are alike. We each build up our individual world as we personify the universal power and presence. What a mystery, and how magnificent!

When we will have learned to be conscious cooperators with the divine creative principle, then our thought will become more concurrent. It stands to reason that we could not have reached this exalted place until we had first learned how to live in harmony with the greater good. But there is nothing restricting about this, since the greater good also includes our individual good.

What we must learn to do is to exercise the authority that the universe has imposed on us and cause the law of Mind to create freedom instead of bondage. This is done by reversing our old order of thought and incorporating a new. We need not destroy anything in our old thought processes which were good; we merely drop out the evil and limiting thoughts, and expand the good. Thus we pass from the old into the new without confusion.

God in the Unlikeable

When we fret ourselves in the presence of an irritating circumstance, we are admitting the presence of something that is *not* a complete expression of God. Thus we perpetuate a false belief that is bound to color our experiences. On the other hand, when we hold to the truth and persist in seeing God in every person or circumstance, then that which is truth is bound to come forth, and we find ourselves becoming conscious heirs of all the good in the universe. To close our eyes to the fact that God is in *everything* in God's universe is to give a false reality to something that is not so. Thus we tend to attract that to which we have given a reality, which in itself it does not have.

A proper understanding of this fundamental fact will wipe out any tendency toward complaining about anything that happens. If everything—every person and every experience—is good, being the expression of the All-Good, then it follows that we must be reading into it something that is not there. In other words, we are reading our false belief into it. And since our beliefs cast their own shadows, we actually see the bad. This confirms our false belief and perpetuates the wrong experience.

If, on the contrary, we have grounded ourselves in the fundamental assumption that God is in that thing or person, then we are able to surround that thing or that person with our love instead of our irritation, and very soon *that which we see comes forth.*

Two people observe Niagara Falls. One says, "Wild horses could never drag me back to this place." The other says, "Marvelous, inspiring, beautiful. I'm coming back every year." The waterfalls are physically the same to both, but one's mental reaction is of distaste and the other's of pleasure. In other words, what we read into any experience colors our reaction to it. Therefore, we should see God in every person and in every experience. This means that we should not allow ourselves to be irritated by anyone, because we cannot become irritated with God.

The Attracting Power of Love

Some time ago a young woman came in for advice. She worked in an office, and the office manager was simply unbearable. She said that in all her life she had never known a person who seemed to take such delight in hurting other people. She enumerated the hundred and one petty meannesses he expressed toward her and others. Finally her irritation toward him reached a point where she hated the way he held his cigar, disliked every tie he wore and was irritated by the very tone of his voice.

What had happened was that she had unified herself only with his negative actions until his voice, clothes, etc. became colored by her unpleasant reactions. When it was pointed out to her that she had no responsibility for his actions, only for her own, she began to see light. She began to say to herself, "What rich, full tones his voice carries. That's a beautiful necktie he has on this morning. Doesn't he smile nicely?" She had taken the first correct step, which was to *eliminate from her own mind* the ugly, un-godlike things she was reading into this person. When she was able to go further and say, "He is an expression of Spirit, made of the same spiritual substance of which I am made, striving for happiness just as I am," she was nearer a good result. It is our *beliefs* that produce our results. Finally she brought herself to say, "How glad I am to be able to work with such a person. I see in him the image and likeness of God. I steadfastly refuse to take note of anything less than this."

As a result of her changed belief, the manager became entirely changed in his attitude. But this is not the most important thing. This woman had found the secret of immunizing herself to irritation by coming to the deep-seated *belief* that God pervades the entire universe. She had learned that "if any say, 'I love God and hate my neighbor,' they are liars, because the neighbor whom they see is merely an expression of God, the unseen." In loving this man, she was bringing herself into line with the Mind of God, which sees only the good.

God Pervades the Body

Very frequently when overtaken by sickness, we fall into a panic of fear. This of course is one of the principal obstructions to spiritual mind healing. We must learn to place our faith in good, transposing the thought of fear into one of faith. It will help us to realize that the body is spiritual substance. It is really some part of the body of God. God pervades it from tip to toe.

In giving mental treatment for physical healing, we should sense the spiritual body. This does not mean that we should try to visualize it, but we should sense it just as we sense the atmosphere of harmony, and we should state that the spiritual body is a reality. We should know that God pervades every cell of the body. We should also know that our recognition and realization of the Divine Presence actually heals. It has the power to dissolve both the wrong thought and its negative manifestation.

If we find ourselves doubting that we have such ability, we should at once affirm that we know what we believe and that we believe what we know. A mental prayer treatment is a series of statements made in Mind for one's self or some other person, or relative to some situation or condition that needs to be changed. This statement in Mind is a clear-cut statement of our belief and should produce a realization in our own thought that the condition that ought to be changed is now being *and has already been* completely changed. To be effective, the treatment must always arrive at a definite conclusion, and if the treatment is to have any healing power, the conclusion at which it arrives must transcend the state of consciousness that produced the negative situation.

Principle of Growth

We should expect to grow in our understanding and use of this law. It is one thing to make a statement of this principle; it is quite a different thing to actually believe. Much of our difficulty comes from the conflict between what we think and what we actually believe deep in consciousness.

If we can catch and hold to the truth that everything in the universe exists for the purpose of aiding our growth and never of stunting or hindering it, we will have evolved a philosophy that will stand the shocks of life. A new attitude will grow out of this new belief. It could be stated as an attitude of relaxation, characterized by the word *let*. The opposite attitude of the past is one of forcing, characterized by the word *must*.

Whenever we are seeking to make a demonstration, we should stop the very moment we find ourselves tensing and trying to force a thing through. This "forcing" is an indication that we recognize the presence of a hostile, opposing power arrayed against us that we must overcome. This is a belief in duality: the presence of God and a supposed opposite—good and evil, health and sickness, prosperity and poverty.

In truth, there is nothing but good in the universe. This good is dedicated to our growth and development. *Nothing* is ever trying to oppose us, and the secret of accomplishment is in *letting* this good come forth. Our part in the work is to rest in this knowledge and to *let* the Universal Mind swing into action. The thing that looks big to us and that leads us into a misguided, tensed "forcing" is infinitesimal to Mind. Being neither person, place or thing, it has no reality. Mind sweeps on in its creative cycle to bring about the greatest growth in the individual.

Most people are afraid of the thing they are fighting. Spirit does not see it; we humans make it large. Spirit knows there is nothing but itself forever expressing through humankind. When we allow this knowledge to enter into the field of our deep belief, we cease struggling and *let* the divine perfection in us stand forth in our experience. By this principle of growth, we will find that our life is characterized by steadily increasing health, happiness and prosperity *without any effort on our part* other than choice and conscious direction.

No Conflict in Mind

Sometimes there is a misunderstanding between two people as a result of angry words or thoughts. When we know that there is only one Mind in the universe, we can relax in the knowledge that there never can be two hostile vibrations in that one Mind, because that Mind knows nothing but oneness. So we treat to heal ourselves of belief in the reality of this difference of opinion. We disregard the apparent break and go back to our fundamental belief that Mind is one; that our mind and the other person's mind are part of the one Mind; that there is a singleness of thought. We steadfastly refuse to talk about or to recognize in any way that which we have been recognizing.

We heal ourselves of any harsh feeling toward others. We do what Jesus suggested: First, become reconciled to your neighbor; and then bring your gift to the altar. This does not mean that we always go to the misunderstanding person and offer reconciliation. But in the secret of our own inner thought, we deliberately remove the hostile feeling, forgive ourselves and the other person, and surround the other person with the universal love of which we both are a part of.

All treatment should be built on this sense of divine unity and oneness with all life. When we say that we heal ourselves of a harsh feeling toward others, we are stating something that is very important in this Science. All healing is self-healing. The thing that distinguishes this Science from most psychological methods of approach is right here. In this method, we practitioners treat ourselves rather than our clients, and yet we treat ourselves *for* our clients.

What are we really doing? We are trying to convince ourselves that those for whom we are working are already both divine and perfect. We are trying to convince ourselves that the circumstances or situations that we are treating are already filled with divine and harmonious action. Those of us who can heal ourselves of the belief that our clients must suffer will generally find a physical improvement in our clients. It is very important to understand this, since it breaks down what otherwise might seem to be barriers and obstacles to one's mental work. This is nothing more than a definite understanding of the meaning of those symbolic words, "You shall know the truth, and the truth shall make you free."

⌒◎

Meditation

God is all there is. I know that there is nothing in the universe except God. My body, my health, my finances, my business are all part of the body of God. God never wishes limitation for God's self, nor could God ever wish me to be limited. God wishes me constantly to express a larger degree of health, happiness and prosperity. I know this.

I now treat myself to heal any belief to the contrary. I know that such belief is a false belief. I treat myself to know in my deepest being that the fullness of God's supply is lavished upon me. I deny the truth of any thought that opposes this. I affirm my belief in the intimate presence of ever-expanding good. In my spirit, I express Spirit. My word is the word of Spirit. My word is the law unto this thing, and I now speak my word to know that I am a complete, unlimited, ever-growing manifestation of God. I do not need to oppose or force anything. I simply let God manifest through me and my affairs. I now direct the law of Mind to make this my fundamental belief. I release my decree unto the law and know that it is so.

⌒◎

Questions

1. Why should we lay a solid foundation for belief?
2. Why do we have a visible universe?
3. How should we view the universe?
4. What enables us to say "Peace be still" to our emotional states?
5. Why should we avoid tenseness in treatment?

Answers

1. We need to lay solid foundations for our beliefs because they are constantly producing results in our experience, regardless of whether they are objectively held or not.
2. The visible universe is the result of the desire of Spirit to express itself in form.
3. We should view the universe as an expression of a living presence, as Spirit in form.
4. We can calm our emotional states by a recognition that Spirit is in all things and does not desire confusion, sickness or limitation.
5. Tenseness in treatment is due to a belief that there is some opposing force. It is a faith in duality, instead of unity.

How Much Can We Expect?

We have been learning about perfect intelligence, perfect law and perfect expectation. But a practical question might arise here, "How much can an apparently imperfect person expect to demonstrate? Should we expect absolute physical perfection, wealth in the millions, flawless happiness, etc.?"

Of course, there must be a sensible and logical answer to such questions. We do not say that just because people think about a million dollars they will receive a million dollars. What we say is, while it is true as far as the principle is concerned that we can have what we wish according to the law of cause and effect, it is also true that no matter what we wish or long for, we will only have what we take. Since the taking is mental, we will only be permitted to take what we are ready to understand. In other words, each one of us will automatically attract to ourselves a physical embodiment of our subjective acceptance of life. This is one of the principal laws of our philosophy, and it is called the law of mental equivalents.

What would be normal for one person might not be normal for another. What one person might regard as normal would possibly stagger the imagination of another by its very bigness. Our standard of expectancy depends entirely on ourselves. The law will see to it that the demonstration will be made at the exact level of this expectancy, this inner mental subjective thought embodiment. Since no one can step out of or away from themselves, it would be impossible for anyone to escape the logic of their own thought.

What Is the Normal Standard?

There is a very pretty song entitled, "Wishing Will Make It So." It sounds encouraging, but it is not true. The world is full of "wishers" who are not "getters." We never get that for which we merely wish. Wishing must be accompanied by and based on a clear understanding of the quality and quantity of good that we normally can expect.

At this point we must understand that we have to reverse much of the world's thought in arriving at a true norm. The world has dropped its eyes to the ground. Hungry for much, it is satisfied with little. Therefore, we must strike out for the heights, away from the mists and fogs of humankind's doubts, and must see things *through the eyes of Spirit.*

Spirit is the only reality. Everything else in our thinking is colored by the relative. If some people have a little better health than others, they are content. If their business is a little better than that of the average person, they are pleased. It they find a fuller measure of happiness than most people, they feel that they are blessed.

These people are making the mistake of measuring their experience by an imperfect standard. Instead of basing their expectancy on the generally limited experience of humankind, they need to found it on an unchangeable basis. The standards of the human race are always in a state of flux, changing from generation to generation, from day to day, and from individual to individual. But the standard of Spirit is ageless, changeless, unvarying. It is perfection, nothing less.

Perfection Is the Normal

When our thinking is divorced from that of the human race and unified with Spirit, our standard changes from that of imperfection to perfection. This is the true norm. Regardless of the experience of the human race, we are all destined for perfection in the minutest detail of our lives.

Spirit could not possibly have any idea that is less than perfection. Anything less than this would be abhorrent to Spirit if it could see it, which it cannot. Spirit sees the perfect and knows nothing of the imperfect. Every step of the great creative activity of Spirit has been characterized by perfection. The tiniest organism is perfectly constructed and functions perfectly at the level of its mechanism.

The blade of grass is a thing of perfection functioning perfectly in its particular sphere. Chemical atoms are things of perfection coming together and separating again according to a perfect law. This same principle is true regarding each one of us, but with one difference. We have gradually built mental states of imperfection, have gazed on them, then have fallen down and worshipped them. Instead of a God of perfection in our imagination, we have created many gods of imperfection, and they are all creatures of our own imagination. *They have no basis in reality.*

Sickness Is Abnormal

Perfect health is the thing we should expect; imperfect health is an abnormality. There is no such thing as a miracle in healing. The healing of a cancer is merely perfection asserting itself. But that healing comes *only* where it is regarded as the true, normal state.

Here we run into mass thought. The past experience of the human race has been one of sickness. We look around and think, "No one ever has escaped the experience of sickness and hardship." Friends say, "It is all right to study this stuff, but don't go and get fanatical over it, or you will end up in the asylum."

The fact is that those who fully expect perfect health are the sanest people in the world. The inmates of an asylum wink and smile at each other when a sane visitor drops in. They feel sure that the sane person is crazy and that they themselves are sane. The world says, "Preposterous!" when one declares that health is normal and sickness is subnormal, but those who look through the eyes of Spirit know that perfection is the sanest, most normal thing in the universe.

Everyone who ever went against the race belief had to do it alone. They told Alexander Graham Bell that it was preposterous to imagine that he could send his voice over a wire. They deemed the steamboat "Fulton's Folly." They sneered at Marconi when he said he could talk without wires. (They had accepted Bell by this time!) They slapped their sides and laughed when anyone dared to stand forth and attempt anything at all that people previously had not been able to do.

So those of us seeking reality must go against the accepted beliefs of the human race if we expect to demonstrate perfection. The mere fact that the human race has supinely accepted sickness and limitation does not prove that there is no way out of this misery. For ages, the human race accepted the cold, fireless world until some intrepid soul struck a spark and started humankind on its way to electrically heated homes. Now the race accepts this as normal and wonders how people could have been so ignorant in the pre-fire days.

What Is the Perfection of Spirit?

We have seen that perfection is the normal experience of Spirit. Therefore, the normal in us is the reproduction in us of what Spirit is in itself. In other words, if Spirit is allowed to reproduce itself in the individual, it will manifest those qualities and characteristics *that it is in itself.*

We have had to find our way to God. We have learned that we are thinkers let loose in the universe, possessed of all the research machinery that will enable us to observe the handiwork of God and thus to find out what God is. There has been no voice from the clouds, no words written by the finger of God on stone, no trance revelation to selected individuals. We have come to know God by observing how God works. We have found much, and we will undoubtedly find more, but at this stage of our evolution we have discovered enough to lead us out into the bright light of perfection. We need only to follow the intuition of our own soul to discover the living presence in the universe.

God Is Life

We know that God is life because the universe is alive. All the manifest universe is indwelt by life. That life is the life of Spirit because there is no other source from which it could possibly come. The true norm for humankind, therefore, is life—life abundant, life to the very fullest extent, unmarred by anything that is touched by death. Spirit is eternal, whole and deathless. In fact, life and death are incongruous because there is nothing except life in Spirit and therefore in its universe. God is life, and the nearer we come to an understanding of this and of our oneness with God, the less we will be subject to anything that limits life, which disease certainly does.

The question might be asked, "Why do we talk so much about God?" The answer is both intelligent and logical. We have already defined God as the intelligent life principle running through everything, the creative power in everything and the Mind at the center of our own being. If, instead of the word *God*, one wishes to say *Life, Creative Principle, Divine Spirit, Universal Soul, Universal Mind,* or just say *It*, the same result would be obtained. The principle thing we have to realize is that Spirit can give us only what we take and that the taking is mental. Next we must understand that mental states become habitual and more or less fixed, although we can always change them. Any mental state that is fixed tends not only to perpetuate itself, but always attracts to itself that which is like itself.

The thing that we change is not the reality or the law, but our own reaction to it. Its reaction to us will always correspond to our reaction to it, just as the reflection in a mirror will always correspond to the image held in front of it. Change the image, and you will change the reflection. Naturally, the more beautiful the image, the more attractive will be its reflection.

We all desire certain things. We would like to be happy. Every normal person wishes to be well, and it is not natural for anyone to desire impoverishment. Surely we all wish love and friendship in our lives, and the cultured mind will desire beauty. Does it seem too good to be true that all of these things are really intended for us? Does it seem like an idle daydream to expect this greater good? Rather, is it not true that something within us by some divine intuition has already told us that all these things belong to us as a part of our natural inheritance? We have listened so long to the suggestions of imperfection that the song of harmony seems unreal.

We must learn to break down the barriers of thought. Expectancy speeds progress, just as joy and enthusiasm give wings to hope. If we practitioners in this Science felt that the statements we made in giving mental treatments were merely repetitions of idle dreams, we would indeed be living in a world of fantasy, flying as it were from one branch of superstition and vain imagination to another. But in reality, there is a deep underlying conviction in every person's mind that life must have a deeper meaning, that goodness must overcome evil, that even death finally must be conquered, and that all that was limiting, all that hurt or that gave pain and suffering must give way to some divine reality. This inner sense is not an illusion. It is not only the guiding star of our hope; it is that without which hope would be impossible.

Should it seem strange that just as we have conquered many of the laws of nature and caused them to do our bidding, just as we have harnessed electricity to the wheels of progress and invention to the comfort of our everyday lives, does it seem strange that there should also be a power or a force in nature finer than electricity and yet just as tangible? A few great souls have appeared throughout the ages who have understood this. They have been the true saviors of humankind.

Moreover, the greatest good that we have ever known has come from their simple teachings.

Every great religion and every great spiritual philosophy has been built on the perception of the few exalted souls who have dared to believe in and trust the universe. Why should we not do likewise? Why shouldn't we develop the God-power within us just as we would any other power? Are not our powers God-powers when they are used in a God-like way?

The creative power of thought is no exception to the general rule of law. It matters not what we have chosen to call it, we are surrounded by a creative intelligence that responds to our word. Since we may consciously shape our word, we may consciously mold our destiny. But we will never do this merely by making a lot of statements about principles or even by saying God is good. God was good before we made the statement. Electrical engineers do more than state their principles. They say there is power in the waterfall, there is energy stored in coal and oil and in the wind and the wave. They announce the existence of a universal energy. It was there before they proclaimed it. It would still be there if they remained ignorant of its nature.

The engineer says that since these energies exist and since we know something of their nature and since we have discovered how to harness them, why not use them? They tell us that there is a definite technique for this use, that there is a way in which this energy is converted into power for definite use.

Jesus, who lived nearly two thousand years ago, proclaimed power and taught that it is always available to those who believe. Because this power exists, prayers have been answered and faith has been justified. But someone might say, "This invisible principle about which you talk so boldly is so vague. Let us weigh and measure it. Let us seek to hold it in our hands and see what it looks like. Let us analyze and dissect it, because we refuse to believe in anything that we cannot objectively touch, taste or handle." What an absurd statement! Who knows how the blush comes to the rose? Did anyone ever weigh and measure the creative principle of life, and yet does any sane person doubt its existence?

The great trouble with human beings is that we haven't yet come to think of the energies of Mind and Spirit in the same natural manner that we think of other energies or laws in nature. Therefore, we have not yet consciously harnessed the power within us to definite purposes. This is what a student of the Science of Mind must learn to do. This process is never a wistful wishing or an idle dreaming. It is an intense reality. The power to live, to create and to expand is already within us, so why not use it? We started this chapter with the assertion that we get not what we wish for, but what we regard as the *normal*. We went on to say that the normal is the reproduction in us of what Spirit is in itself. Since Spirit is life, we should take time to meditate quietly at this point on our own inner expectation and to find out how much life we can mentally embody and accept, because this and this alone is what we will manifest. An imperfect concept of life means an imperfect demonstration; a perfect concept of life means a perfect manifestation.

God Is Truth

We found in an earlier lesson that a lie is something that is not true, and truth is that which *is*. God knows nothing that does not exist. Everything that God knows exists. God does not know limitation; therefore there is no limitation. God does not know poverty; therefore there is no poverty. God does not know unhappiness; therefore there is no unhappiness. God knows nothing negative *at all*. God knows only that which is positive. Therefore, those of us unifying ourselves with God look through the eyes of God, and no matter what our old vision seeks to tell us, we close our spiritual eyes to it and affirm *only the good*.

Meditation

God is the light. In God is no darkness at all. In the consciousness that God is light and that I am one with God, I become aware that all around me is bright and clear. The way is perfected by this interior light and consciousness of truth.

God is peace. God is not the author of confusion, but of peace. There is a fundamental harmony in the universe, and I am one with that harmony. Confusion is an experience of humankind, not a condition of God thought.

God is power. I am one with God; therefore power sweeps through me resistless, unyielding and unopposed. I speak my word, and this irresistible power takes it and brings into my experience as manifestation, the substance of my thought.

God is perfection. God is whole and complete. Since I am some part of God, this perfection is now my real experience. God as light, peace, power and perfection is the very substance of my life and being. I rest quietly in this knowledge, and all is well with me.

❧

Questions

1. Can we get what we wish by the use of the Science of Mind?
2. What is the difference between the standard that we have accepted as ours and the standard of Spirit?
3. How can we change our accepted standard?
4. Why do we assert that God is life?
5. What do we mean by the word *God*?

Answers

1. We get only as much of what we wish as we are able to take. We can take only what we can subjectively embody.

2. The standard accepted by us as a result of experience changes from generation to generation. The standard of Spirit is changeless perfection.

3. We change our standard by unifying with Spirit. In the process of unification, the perfection of the spiritual reality is substituted for our imperfect standard.

4. We claim that God is life because we find the whole manifest universe indwelt by life, and there is no other source for it except Spirit, God.

5. By *God* we mean creative principle or first cause, Divine Mind, Universal Soul, the self-conscious principle of the universe that works through impersonal law.

How Spirit Manifests through Us

In the previous chapter, we stated that the law of Mind will produce anything for us provided we first embody the idea and meaning of that thing. By embodiment, we do not mean merely wishing. We mean actual, conscious and subjective acceptance of the meaning of an idea. Since Spirit is life, love and peace, and since it also must be harmony, one cannot expect to embody spiritual ideas through hatred, confusion or greed. Spiritual ideas must be spiritually discerned.

We are handicapped in arriving at spiritual realization because of the race belief in imperfection, and it does not necessarily follow that what one person considers normal would be normal to another. No one can expect to demonstrate beyond their ability to rise in consciousness to a complete comprehension of the meaning of the idea they wish to embody. Naturally, an absolute standard of normalcy could be complete perfection. Anything less than this would not be normal to the Spirit. Each of us should seek to know deep within ourselves that perfection is possible, and in working out our problem we should realize that our claim to imperfection is conditioned by the accumulated race belief inherited from previous generations, plus the effect of the thought atmosphere around us. To realize this is to understand where most of the arguments for imperfection come from. Hence, we are saved from gloom while striving for mastery when we know that the thought that seeks to limit us arises not from nature, but from the mind of humankind.

How We Develop

There is a law of perfection constantly seeking to manifest through us, but we furnish imperfect conditions through which it must manifest. Since this law is always neutral and impersonal, it can manifest for us only through the kind of mental vehicle we furnish for it. The law provides the power; we furnish the conditions.

Naturally, different types of people furnish different vehicles through which this infallible law operates. The law completely ignores personal peculiarities and idiosyncrasies. It makes no distinctions between individuals, but operates always on the mental concept set before it. The law never shuts anyone out. It includes all people. We are liable to think that because others differ from us, the law of Spirit excludes them from reaching their desires until they shift their way of thinking to more nearly meet our opinions. Yet, the very person whose exterior may grate on us may easily be a more perfect vehicle for the operation of law than we are ourselves.

Students of the Science of Mind should be tolerant. We should be able to meet all sorts and conditions of people on their own levels, looking through external differences to the inner sameness and loving everybody because each person is an expression of Spirit. If the Spirit is peace, we should not permit ourselves to become irritated by others. Nor should we withdraw from people because their habits of life are different from ours. The Spirit never withdraws from anyone.

We must not forget that ideals of living change, more or less, in each age. That which the mass consciousness of one generation regarded as wicked and evil, the following generation often seeks to emulate. A few years ago a man walking down the street with a twenty dollar gold piece in one hand and a bottle of whiskey in the other would have been arrested for the possession of the whiskey. Today he would still be arrested, but it would be for the possession of the gold. This is not written to advocate the use of the whiskey, but rather to show that the human standard of values changes. The person of whom we disapproved twenty years ago may have become our closest friend today. The world of opinion is a rapidly changing one, and we will arrive at no stable foundation until we realize the unchanging nature of reality in the spiritual universe in which we live.

Source of Power

We continuously draw on Spirit as the source of our power. Mind is the agency through which this power flows and from which it emanates. Mind is power, and power is Mind. There is no necessity for pleading, begging or agonizing. We merely *recognize* power and open the consciousness to the very fullest capacity to receive it and to allow it to flow.

When we recognize that Spirit saturates every atom in the universe and, incidentally, flows into our own body, business, home and all our external affairs, then we are able to realize that this source of life is sending power through all these experiences by and through the law of Mind. It is the Spirit at the very center of all life that we must train to perceive and accept.

The race belief sometimes asserts itself at this point to raise a doubt, saying, "Perhaps Spirit might not give this power." This is a carryover from an older theological belief, the belief that God gives to one and withholds from another for some inscrutable reason. We must rid ourselves of this notion. We must know that the law of Mind carrying all the power in the universe is entirely neutral, exerting itself whenever it is directed and pouring forth unstinted at our decree. There is no need of coercion, nor need there be any feeling of hesitance as to whether it will be there when we need it. It *will* be there, never fear. Our part is merely to set the law in motion through our spoken word. Coupled with this should be an attitude of expectancy of its activity as a normal procedure. At first there may be something of timidity as we begin to do definite work. But gradually as we find the law swinging into action in the direction we have indicated, we come to *know*, where formerly we merely *hoped*.

The law of Mind is the surest thing in the universe. Our hopes may change; the law never changes. It knows only one thing: to obey the voice of Spirit. This truth will bear repetition, because it is fundamental. So take time to ponder deeply this fact. On it rests your entire success in making conscious use of the law of Mind.

Not Occupied with Details

Do not be over occupied with the details of the manner in which the law is to work. Simply see the power resistlessly sweeping on to a triumphant conclusion. Rest and relax in this assurance, and leave to Mind the exact details as to how it is to operate, because it knows exactly how to go about following your directions.

Too often, beginners want to stipulate and outline the exact method by which Spirit should operate. This is not wise, because Mind has infinite resources of which we have scarcely had a glimpse, and in carrying out the work to a successful conclusion, it may draw on a number of unforeseen forces and bring the answer through channels undreamed of by the one who has set the law in motion.

Positive Drives Out Negative

The successful practitioner knows that the thing on which the thought dwells tends to become objectified in one's experience. Hence, we should never dwell too much on anything that is negative. Jesus healed disease by a contemplation of perfect health and by an inner sense of certainty that health is normal and natural. He dissipated want through the realization of complete supply. He obliterated hate by refusing to permit it entrance into his consciousness and by dwelling on the idea of infinite love. He said, "Do good to them that hate you." When we dwell too much on negative thoughts, we unify with their rate of vibration and bring into our experience the very thing from which we seek to be freed. Somewhere in a proper mental treatment, we must arrive at the conviction that Spirit is all, that it is supreme. Hate is conquered by love, even as fear becomes dissolved in faith. Nor should we feel that we are arraying one power against another.

Spirit Sees Only Itself

Spirit has only one mode of action, which is self-contemplation. It sees only itself, never anything else. It knows nothing outside of itself. If it did, it would be creating two things and we would have duality in the universe. This belief in duality is responsible for all the devils, Satans, inquisitions and witch-burnings because it is a belief in both good and evil. Spirit sees only the good, because it sees and knows nothing but itself.

Spirit passes into many different forms, it is true, but no matter what the form, it is always its own self. We therefore look beyond the form to the inner reality and know it to be good. Thus we can look into the face of some apparently horrible situation and see nothing but God there. In this way we rob it of its fearsomeness. In physical healing, we never shudder and say, "My, that *is* bad, or serious, or incurable, or repulsive." Instead, we see the divine presence and perfection in the client, and it is there because that perfection is the normal standard and is always present.

The Unfailing Law

The question is often asked, "Did God make the law of Mind?" The answer is self-evident. The law of Mind has always existed. It is the mode of action of the Divine Nature, and this law can never fail to operate. This is the secret power of faith, a complete realization that the law of Mind must work.

God as Spirit is the divine presence always stimulating our thought. The law of Mind, obeying the will of this divine presence, has no choice of its own. We need never ask, "Does God wish us to enjoy health, happiness and abundance, or to live the good life?" The very fact that the Divine Nature is one of perfection and of wholeness presupposes the necessity that this Divine Nature wishes us everything that is good. The law of Mind, being neutral, never argues against our desire, but always seeks to fulfill it. Therefore, when our thought is in accord with the Divine Harmony and when we have complete faith and conviction in its power, then there will be no question whatsoever about the operation of the law.

Law must always move along the line of our thought. It merely becomes necessary that we understand the meaning of the truth Jesus referred to when he told us that there is a truth that automatically works for us when we understand it. But there should be no mental reservation in our acceptance of this truth. We must weed out everything from the mentality that denies the power of our word to demonstrate the truth. We should seek a complete acceptance of the power of our word, and this acceptance is not complete until it becomes subjective. We will know when it has become subjective, because when this desired result does take place, there will no longer be anything in us that denies the good that our word affirms.

In doing this we should make every endeavor to free ourselves from any sense of strain or anxiety. To make known our requests with thanksgiving is a scientific approach to reality. We should seek to develop a childlike trust and a complete simplicity in approaching both the law and Spirit. The law is not made to cooperate with us by the use of many words, but rather cooperates with us because of the meaning we give to the words we use. Anatole France, a master of words, was once asked, "How short can a sentence be and still be effective?" His answer was, "One word, if you can do it." So one word spoken with the deep realization of its meaning is better than thousands of words rattled off without any meaning.

If we use the phrase "God *is* and is all there is" relative to any particular circumstance, and if this idea that God is all there is seems hazy in our thought, we must continue to meditate on it until we sense its meaning. The idea must be clear before the law can make it into a concrete and tangible result in our experience. Never forget that you are dealing with an immutable law of cause and effect, and that what you do when you give a treatment is to change some tendency in this law—some sequence of events—by introducing a realization of life that automatically dissolves the old sequence and as automatically sets a new one in motion. In doing this you are not destroying, neutralizing or obliterating the law itself; you are merely using it in a different way.

Face the Problem Today

Our future is being created out of our present concepts, just as our present experiences are largely a result of what has gone before. Hence, if there is any problem that confronts us at this moment, we should face it immediately. That which we set in motion today becomes the experience of tomorrow, but it can never become a fact in our experience unless we first take the specific and definite steps to start it on its way. The future is merely the lengthened shadow of today. It is one with today. It is born out of today. The bright and happy tomorrows of which we dream must not be thought of as though the imagination conceived them to be something that is about to take place, but must become a part of our mental acceptance of the today in which we live.

We have been told that when we pray we must believe that we already possess what we are praying for. This is a definite statement of the law of cause and effect and most certainly is a scientific approach to demonstration.

⌒

Meditation

I am aware that there is a potent power available to me for any and every use I wish to make of it. My Spirit, recognizing the unity of humankind and God, can desire nothing opposed to the good of the whole, because the hurt of another is my hurt. I know that there is a limitless abundance of good available in the universe, and I now quietly, definitely and expectantly announce my need and its fulfillment.

I know that there is no problem facing me that is a problem from the standpoint of all-knowing, all-intelligent Spirit. I therefore announce that the answer to my so-called problem, now known subjectively, is made known where it needs to be in order that my complete and definite good may come to me.

Questions

1. Is the law a respecter of persons?
2. Why should we refuse to permit ourselves to be irritated with others?
3. What is the source of power?
4. Do we need to fear that Spirit will withhold power when we seek it?
5. Why should we refuse to hold negative thoughts?

Answers

1. The law is no respecter of persons. It makes no distinction between individuals, but operates on the mental concepts each individual sets before it.
2. We should not permit ourselves to be irritated with others, because each one of us is an expression of Spirit, and Spirit is peace.

3. Spirit is the source of power, and Mind is the agency for its operation.

4. We need never fear that God will withhold anything from us. Power is available always, a neutral impersonal force always flowing in the direction that is decreed for it by the word of any person.

5. We should refuse to hold negative thoughts, because that on which we dwell in thought tends to become objectified in our experience.

Mystics and Intellectuals

❧

Students of the Science of Mind should understand that there are different approaches to truth. Moreover, we should be able to discriminate between them and to know which approach we are using at any particular time. The scientist, the religionist and the philosopher are all endeavoring to find the true bases on which the universe rests. Yet all approach the problem from a slightly different angle. As students of the Science of Mind, we approach this understanding from a combination of all three.

Religionists, facing the problem from the point of view of revelation, search along the pathways of "revealed truth" and arrive at the conclusion that there is a universal intelligence to which or to whom they give the name *God*. Philosophers, following the pathway of abstract reasoning, give to this intelligence the name *reality*. Scientists, working through observation, experiment and test, arrive finally at what they call a *principle*. So, from widely divergent points of approach, all feel or find their way back to a universal intelligence, or first cause.

The methods by which they arrive are likewise different. Scientists use cold intellect, religionists use mystical sense, and philosophers use a combination of the two. All methods are good, whether of pure mental and intellectual activity or of the higher spiritual intuition. All help to fill in the gaps left in the others' results.

The Mystic's Approach

Mystics are those who have a deep inner sense of life and of their unity with the whole. Mysticism has nothing to do with the mysterious. A mystic is not necessarily a psychic. Some are, but many more are not. A person may have psychical experiences that may be either real or the product of the imagination, but the experience that the mystic has is always real. Mystics have given to the world the very highest that we have in philosophy, religion, literature in general and poetry in particular. Mystics are those who intuitively perceive truth and, without conscious mental process, arrive at spiritual realization. No one could have been their teacher, because they proclaim truth never before enunciated. They must have had direct contact with Spirit and received the truth through an intuitive process. They were taught not of people, but of God.

It is as though mystics have withdrawn from the harsh, conflicting voices of the world into a deeper world of their own inner being, have contacted there the divine that is in everyone, have seen the light that lights everyone that comes into the world, have laid their true selves open to the presence within, have looked into the face of God and have come forth speaking things that never were heard on land or sea. Yet all have uttered their message from reality in such a way that, when taken together, form a composite whole.

The founders of most of the great religions were mystics. The great poets whose works have lived on were all mystics. From the author of Job through Tennyson to Walt Whitman, the ever-living poets have been deeply conscious of the all-pervading presence of God. They seem to walk always in the shadow of a living presence that they are trying to express and which, if they are indeed great poets, they do express. Reading their words, one is conscious of an indefinable "something" that saturates those words, and the soul of the reader is stilled by the call of that presence and sweetened by its fragrance.

The Teaching of the Mystics

Mystics teach that the Divine Presence is real and that there should be a conscious courting of that Presence. It indwells not only humans, but the rocks, the trees, the flowers, the whole visible universe, and there should be a conscious balanced receptivity to it and a recognition of it in everything seen, heard or felt. This teaching of a spiritual universe, which is nothing more nor less than a living Presence, is the secret of the mystics. They have not contacted it through the intellect; they have rather *felt* and *experienced* it.

Jesus, for example, said in effect to the intellectual teachers of his time, "You teach things that you have heard from others, but I speak *that which I know.*" After all, all that we can possibly know about God is that which we directly experience.

When Jesus said he taught that which he had known and seen, he was on the strongest possible ground, because he was able to demonstrate that his were no idle words. He taught a triumphant, absolute, transcendent law, and he taught that this law *heals by its very presence.* He did not dispute with people; he demonstrated the law and let it speak for itself. When they asked him by what power he did these things, he answered, "The Creator that dwells in me does the works."

He knew intuitively that God is indivisible, that the Infinite cannot be divided against itself. It can be nothing less than a complete unit. Since we are all a part of this great Whole, we never are nor can be separated from God. Further, he knew at a glance that God is present at every point. Outwardly, he walked and talked with people; inwardly, he talked with the Creator. He was subject to the terrific assault of the world thought on his mentality, but he lived withdrawn in the deep center of his being, holding this part of his being open to the infilling Presence. When the pressure became particularly great, he went alone to some secluded place and there recaptured his deep vision of the absolute oneness of God and humankind.

Mystics and Realization

All mystics have given the same message, that all manifestation of life is from an invisible to a visible plane, from the inner to the outer, from the image to the concrete. They have taught that *we must unify our own mentality with pure Spirit.* This is done not through labor and struggle, rather its opposite. There must be a deep awareness of the Creator within and a steadily growing realization of one's complete unity with the Creator. When we arrive at the point where we can say and really *feel* as an unalterable fact that "I and my Creator are one," we can do mighty works, because then we recognize the fact that when we speak, Spirit speaks, and that we need not raise our voice to get results, because all the power of that irresistible Presence flows in the direction of our word.

Mysticism and Authority

This intimate sense of the indwelling Presence colored every word that Jesus spoke and every act he performed. It invested his words and actions with an authority before which even the power of the Roman Empire had to give way. When the soldiers were sent out to arrest him, they returned empty-handed, and when asked for an explanation they said, "Never anyone spoke like this one." His time had not yet come. When it did come and he was arrested in the garden of Gethsemane, he said (and he *knew* it to be true) that he could have called in spiritual assistance that would have prevented his arrest. When the insane person, from whom sane people ran, faced him quietly and with the complete assurance, he commanded the insane condition to cease. When the elements hurled the tiny cockleshell of a boat on the crest of the waves and its passengers were in terror, he rose up and commanded the storm, "Peace. Be still." There was an authority there that came from his positiveness regarding the inner Presence, which he recognized at all times and under all circumstances.

Finally, when he stood before Pilate, he completely overshadowed him. A stranger picture never was seen. On the one side sat Pilate, surrounded by a splendor that must have been awesome in itself and backed by all the power of the Roman Empire. The people cringed before Pilate, knowing his cruel, sadistic nature. Yet Jesus looked him in the eye fearlessly. He, the prisoner dressed in plain garb, hands bound, was condemned already in the wicked brain of Pilate. Yet as he stood facing this earthly ruler, his face bore an expression of level benignity which Pilate was unaccustomed to find in prisoners. There was a calmness and assurance, an evident air of authority that Pilate felt. There was not the slightest tendency toward panic. Jesus stood there looking through the shriveled soul of the ruler. In his silent authority, he was "every inch a sovereign."

Pilate became nervous, then irritable, and finally to break the spell, he almost shrieked "Speak!" Jesus had imposed a higher authority on Pilate, and the watchers saw him shrink as Jesus stood there majestic in his calm. Remember, Jesus was just one person with no organization to back him up, no political "pull," no way out but through death by torture. But such was his consciousness of the divine Presence within that it brushed aside the power of a mighty world empire as though it did not exist.

This is the kind of authority the mystic has. It may never have to be exerted against the state, but it has to be daily used against the forces of disease and death. There must be the same deep consciousness of unbreakable unity with the whole, the assured knowledge that the entire presence of the Divine is within, otherwise panic will rule in the presence of some appearance of discord, and the day will be lost. On the other hand, when we know and "feel" that we are one with a power that is triumphant, absolute and transcendent, against which all lesser laws mean nothing, we are able to stand face to face with life's most terrible appearances and impose our authority on them. Then, conscious of the indissolubility of this union, we incorporate this consciousness in our word, and then our word has power because we realize that we are in God and God is in us.

Weakness of Mere Intellect

Pure intellectuals never know the joy of such an experience. They know only that which they can set forth in mathematical equation. Beyond this, they are afraid to go. But we take their reasoned deductions and sound conclusions and, adding them to our intuitive perceptions, round out our philosophy.

The world is filled with students of philosophy who have allowed their intellectual grasp of truth to outdistance their inner mystical apprehension. Anyone can study facts, store them in memory and carry on a clear-thinking discussion of them, but this is far from knowing their value. It is one thing to "hold the truth," but it is a different thing to let the truth hold you.

Be watchful against this common tendency toward a merely intellectual understanding of the Science of Mind. Remember, we have two aspects of truth: the inner and the outer. It is imperative that we develop this inner side of life; the outer will then take care of itself. Spend time in quiet meditation on this central fact, the fact that you who are reading these lines are just as surely indwelt by the Divine Presence as Jesus was; that every bit of energy that was available to Jesus is also available to you; that God is not one inch farther away from you than God was from Jesus, because God is in you at this moment and is there in God's entirety. *All of the presence of God is in you at this moment.* It does not matter how you feel. You may think yourself insignificant, ignorant of the truth and not possessed of any great gift. Yet you have the greatest gift in the world, the Divine Presence within you, filling your consciousness if you wake up to the realization of it. To the degree that you know this and get the "feel" of it, you will have power.

In meditation for demonstration, we should allow this truth

to completely saturate our mentality, not merely as an intellectual concept, but rather as a living fire, a moment by moment reality. The Divine Presence fills every atom of the body and flows through every condition and situation that you will confront. The ability to bring this Divine Presence into objective manifestation depends on your inner sense of assurance that the dynamic power and the Divine Presence already are. To cultivate this sense of omnipresence and to realize the power accompanying it is, of course, the secret of successful demonstration. Demonstration means bringing some particular good into your life that you have not been experiencing, or bringing it into the life of some other person.

The question might arise at this point, "Do we have a right to use spiritual power for material purposes?" The logical answer to this question is that there is no such thing as a material purpose in itself, because everything is shot through with pure Spirit. We certainly have the right to use the power of Mind for any purpose that more completely expresses life. The whole criterion should be, "Does the purpose for which I seek to use this power promote physical, mental and spiritual well-being? Does it make people whole and happy? Does it add to the world's sense of joy without harming anyone?" If so, it must be in line with the Divine Nature.

Everyone senses God at the center of their own being. Everyone actually realizes power, but not everyone has learned how to use their spiritual power for definite purposes. This is what the Science of Mind teaches us, to harness the dynamic energy of Mind to our thought patterns. This is done by first knowing that the power is there, and then by definitely using this power for specific purposes.

In your mental work, you should not only say, "God is the only Mind there is," but you must also add that since God is the only Mind there is, then God is the Mind you are using. God is the Mind of your client, the intelligence governing your client's affairs. It is daily guiding the client, causing the right decisions to made. Merely making abstract statements will never do this. We must consciously speak the word if we expect definite results. That is, we must connect our thought with the idea of Spirit in action. Power undirected will never do anything. Spiritual and mental power are no different from other powers; they are merely higher or more intense powers.

༄

Meditation

Today I am aware that the Spirit which indwells me is the Spirit of God. In Spirit, I live and move and have my being, and Spirit lives and moves and expresses itself in me. I know, then, that since this inner Spirit is God, there is a place within me—in the beyond that is within—where I am identified with the invincible power of the universe. The power in me is the power of God, limitless, always expanding in my experience as I recognize that the Creator that dwells in me—the Creator who constitutes my "me"—does the works. I am therefore calm, unconfused and assured as I speak my word for improved health and greater abundance for daily living, because I am speaking not from the standpoint of an individual alone, but I speak from the vantage ground of my oneness with the infinite Spirit and know that all that the Creator has is mine.

༄

Questions

1. Name three approaches to truth.
2. What is a mystic?
3. What have the mystics taught?
4. What do we mean when we say that we have "an inner and an outer aspect of truth"?
5. What is the meaning of the saying, "Everything is shot through with pure Spirit"?

Answers

1. Science, religion and philosophy are three different ways of approaching truth.
2. Mystics are those who perceive truth intuitively. They may test their truth by thought (philosophy) or by experience (science).
3. Mystics have taught that there is one Presence that indwells all things, both the sentient creation and the inorganic universe.
4. By the inner side of life, we mean the indwelling Spirit that maintains the form. By outer, we mean the world of manifestation. There is no outside without an inside, and no inside without an outside.
5. When we say that "everything is shot through with pure Spirit," we mean that the physical universe is ultimately Spirit.

Making Good Come Forth

The Science of Mind can be applied to every department of our activity. People sometimes say that while they can see how the mind can control the body and its states of health, they cannot feel the same confidence in regard to business, the sale of property, profit in investments and such financial activities as are common to our economic setup. This is a false notion that must be replaced by the certainty that Mind operates in everything that goes on in the universe.

The error in many instances is due to carrying over certain concepts from more restricted religious thinking. Older theology taught that God singled out certain people and poured into their lives great riches, honor, fame and what is known as "success." Toward others, God adopted a different attitude in which God withheld these things for some reason that we could not fathom. These people probably worked just as hard, were just as sincere and honest, yet things continually went wrong. Just at the time when they had struggled out from under a load of debt and could see daylight ahead, some unforeseen sickness, with its attendant hospital or doctor bills, would come along and fling them back under the load once more. If they managed to battle their way out of this situation, the next upset would be that they would lose their jobs. If they managed to save a little money and invest it, the investment would fail.

Ignorant of the law of Mind, the theologian had no other answer to this tragic situation than "God willed it so" and that our duty in this event was to resign ourselves to the will of God, accept our hard lot and try to "grow spiritually."

Years of thinking along any one line will leave their mark, and one of the things we must do is to divorce our present thinking from any of the older ideas that tend toward limitation. God's will is for an ever-increasing demonstration of the good things of life. Health is just as material an activity as money-making, and if God-Mind can be called in to promote a person's health, it can just as truly and confidently be trusted to promote a bank account.

Property Is Spiritual

Recently a new property owner came in for assistance. He had saved his money and bought a bungalow court. He had figured the income that the rentals would bring in, deducted the interest, taxes and other expenditures that would be necessary, and after allowing for an occasional vacancy, he still had projected a nice living for himself.

But after acquiring ownership, things turned out other than he had planned. The property was very difficult to rent. Tenants moved out and few came in response to his advertising. He spent larger sums for advertisements, but still the renters stayed away. It looked as if he would lose the place. He said to me, "When I leave you today, I wish didn't have to go back to the deadness of the place. I have come to hate the very sight of it."

During the conversation, it developed that he doubted very much if God cared whether he rented the place or not. He said, "I have tried to believe it, but I cannot pray with assurance, because, after all, God might want me to lose the property for some hidden reason." It was called to his attention that there must first of all be a clear understanding of the spiritual nature of property.

The earth was an earlier manifestation of God than human beings were. The earth was formed as the abode of its coming inhabitants and was so constructed as to provide them with sustenance. This part of the body of God is as spiritual as any other and must be so understood. When it was brought into form, it was *good*. Anything that God makes *is good*.

Working Together with God

There must be the realization that we are co-workers with God. We are dealing with the formed earth, which we recognize as the body of God, and we are one with God in our mastery of the earth. Everything in the universe harmoniously exists for the good of every other part, so the earth certainly is not withholding its cooperation. We tell it to bring forth substance for us—as farmers sow, so they may reap. That sustenance might be in the form of crops or it might be in the form of buildings. If we make a living through rentals or the sale of property, we have as much right to expect success as the farmer does. Therefore, we work together with God to make this land produce a living, good crop of rentals.

The property owner was also told that he must substitute love for hate. He had come to hate the property, the body of God. We mentally separate ourselves from anything we hate, so he was separating himself from God through his feelings against the property. It was suggested that he tell the property how much he loved it and that he take the necessary time to induce within himself this deep-seated love for the property not necessarily as a bringer of income, but first and foremost as a part of God's body.

It was explained to him that there must be an acceptance of the fact that the law of Mind works as readily in this thing as it does in the matter of healing; that it can be directed to bring him the people who need this property, want it, like it and have the money to pay for it. He must love these people before he ever meets them and know that they will enjoy living in this particular spot. When the thought arose of "It is a poor renting locality," he must immediately substitute the conviction of "This is a good locality, very desirable for those whom Mind brings to it. They like it for special reasons that are not recognized by others who pass it by. I know that the property is rented in Mind at this moment. God knows it to be good, and I affirm that it is good."

See the Deal Completed

Just as we are able to look backward by calling on memory and bringing people and incidents out of the past into the present, so Mind is able to bring people and incidents from the future into the present. Mind knows no past, no future, only the *now*. Therefore, all good is complete right now. It is here now. Mind has rented those apartments *now* to someone whom the owner has not yet met, and thanks is given for this accomplished fact.

As the owner induced this inward conviction that the apartments are already rented, a change was produced in his mental state. He no longer worried over the question, "Will this be rented?" Rather, he said, "I know it is rented. I wonder if this is the person to whom Mind has already rented it. If that person does not take it, then I know that this person is not the one, and instead of being depressed and discouraged, I look expectantly toward the coming of the next one, knowing that this one surely is coming to inquire, see it, like it and take it, paying me a fair price for it."

Instead of thinking, "I hope I can persuade someone. I'll promise anything to get them in. I'll cut the rent or make other concessions, because they may be the only ones who look at it," he said, "This place has a value, is fairly priced and is exactly what is wanted by the one to whom Mind already has rented it." Thus he constantly looked beyond the tenant to the Giver. He was friendly and grateful and happy toward the renter, but always in Mind he was going beyond this person to the real source of his supply.

This is what Jesus tried to impress on us when he said to those who were tensed and strained by their fears that they would not have enough to eat, drink or wear, "Seek *first* the realm (inner awareness) of God and God's righteousness, and all these other things will be added unto you." Always look beyond the channel to the source.

Subsequently, five people moved into the property owner's place. They were from a construction crew that was to start digging a flood control channel in the neighborhood. They moved their families into all but one of the vacant apartments. Three days later, an elderly couple from the East moved in, and the eight apartments were filled. The ditch-digging job ended at about the same time that the Easterners left for their home. By this time, a trucking and contracting company moved its business into the neighborhood. The drivers and helpers rented the apartments, and the owner has since learned that God's will is not limitation, but full complete expression. He has learned that Mind operates in the field of finance just as surely as in that of health.

Material and Spiritual Are One

The same underlying philosophy operates in the field of business. Property, goods and services may have all the appearance of materiality, yet to those who understand the spiritual and mental origin of the universe, they are spiritual and mental. Too many people interested in metaphysics follow the accepted standards of the mass-thought. They separate things into spiritual and material. Most property owners think in terms of material, such as size and location of the lot, the physical type and quality of the buildings, nearness to transportation, measured earning power, the fact that more modern property is nearby, etc.

Students of Science of Mind do not throw these proven fundamentals of business to one side. We study all of them, recognize them, and are very careful to conform our investment to rules of good business. Yet we realize that the control of the situation is mental and spiritual. We recognize nothing in the material that can hinder the free flow of Mind in and through our business, and we thereby invest our property with something more than the mere physical appeal on which a bank would loan money, that is, facts and figures that can be set down and analyzed on paper. We add to the property a spiritual quality that is more real than all the balance sheets and is the drawing power that leads people to want to live there, even though they might not fully understand what it is that makes them so decide.

Why Some Businesses Succeed

Some businesses carry that certain "something" that draws people to them. That "something" is the inner consciousness of the owner or manager. All business is the inner consciousness of the owner or the one in charge. Business never grows by accident or luck. Those people who *know*, and know that they know, who have a proper understanding of the real nature of money and build it into their inner consciousness, will do better business than those who do not. This is flatly final because it is *truth*.

Vendors who apply this principle will sell more goods. They cannot fail to do so. It is the law. Having selected a line of goods to sell, a line that has merit, that is fairly priced (though not necessarily the cheapest) and that fills a need in society, they can, using honest, square methods of merchandising, sell very profitable quantities of their produce through good and bad times, as long as they keep "bad times" out of their own consciousness.

When we know deeply within ourselves that there is only one Mind, and that the mind of our prospects, our own mind and Universal Mind are all one; when we know that our goods are nothing less than Mind condensed into tangible form; when we recognize that the amount of our sales are determined *within ourselves* and that we first form these sales as a mental concept within our own consciousness, that as they are firmly established in Mind they will assuredly take form because they *are* Mind in form, then our sales will mount.

We Contribute to the Social Order

Each of us is constructed along different lines. We all, because of these differences in power, temperament and mental outlook, have something different to contribute to humankind. Never waste time envying that which other people seem to have. You have something that they do not have. If all people had what everyone else had, it would hold no value in the world because there would be nobody to whom it would be a contribution. An army consists of soldiers, engineers, radio operators and cooks. Since all contribute their particular specialty, their harmonious cooperation enables the army to move forward as a unit.

So in the one Mind, each of us with our own peculiar mental slant is fulfilling the purpose of life. As we make our individual contribution to the social order, we are fulfilling the purpose of the High Command, and we can be sure that others will contribute to our good. This is the law of the universe. We have every right to expect that our contribution will in turn draw to us ample supply, high success and an ever-increasing expression of the all-good. Only one person in the entire universe can hinder you from accomplishing this, and that person is *you.*

Since you are the only one who can hinder the desired result from taking place in your experience, it naturally follows that your entire mental treatment is given in your own mind. This is one of the all-important points in demonstrating the Science of Mind. It means that *all treatment is self-treatment.* If the Spirit is already willing and if the law must obey, it logically follows that the demonstration must first take place in the minds of the those giving the treatment, whether they are working for themselves or someone else.

It is indeed fortunate that this is so, or else we should all be compelled to admit that destiny is outside the self. Unless there is a power within the self that, when consciously used, produces definite results, there would be no Science of Mind and no spiritual universe available for our use. Whoever said "Be still, and know that I am God" must have perceived this. All treatment is self-treatment, and as far as you are concerned in using this law, you will never have anyone to convince but yourself.

How necessary it is, then, that you become fully convinced not only of the Divine Presence, but of the supremacy of the law! The way to successfully treat is to work with your own thought until you yourself believe what you have stated. This may take one moment, one hour, one day, one week, one month, one year. No one can answer this for you but yourself. Your self merges with the Great Self and is one with the only power in the universe, but you must consciously use this power if you expect definite results. Again, power unused will do nothing. You must recognize spiritual power and then use it.

∽∾

Meditation

There is only one substance in the universe. This substance is co-eternal with God and is the medium of God's manifestation in the external world. I now recognize that this eternal spiritual substance flows into my body as physical perfection and into the body of my affairs as supply. I know that there is no will of God compelling me to suffer lack, limitation or distress in mind, body or estate. The invisible goodness is now my bountiful supply.

∽∾

Questions

1. Is limitation an expression of the "will of God"?
2. Why are material possessions classed as a part of the "body of God"?
3. Why should we keep "bad times" out of our consciousness?
4. If we are unsuccessful, on whom does the blame rest?

5. When we give a treatment, whom do we seek to convince of the truth of our statements?

Answers

1. God's will, being God's nature, can never be in the direction of limitation. It must be in line with the enlargement of self-expression.
2. Since we think of the world of manifestation as the body of God, then material possessions, being a part of the manifest world, must be classed as a part of the body of God.
3. We should keep "bad times" out of our minds because what we hold within the consciousness tends to manifest outward experience. To believe that times are bad will make them hard for the one who so believes.
4. If anyone is unsuccessful—no matter how many alibis they may provide—the blame really lies with themselves through their ignorance and misuse of the law of cause and effect.
5. When we give a treatment, we are not attempting to convince a client, a prospective buyer or a sick person. We are convincing ourselves of the truth of such statements as we may make.

THE SENSE LIFE AND THE INNER LIFE

A question that arises sooner or later in the mind of any thoughtful student of this Science is, "If we are created in the image and likeness of God and must therefore have been created perfect, how then did we come to develop our negative attitude?" The fact is, we are endowed with one quality that even God cannot violate. We are endowed with *will*, just as Spirit is. We have the power of choice, a power that carries a terrific responsibility but also a glorious opportunity. We have been subjectively carried along by a universal creative activity until we reached the stage where will, reason and the power of choice emerged. From then on, we are free to choose that which we wish. This power of free choice saves us from being robots. We cannot imagine that Spirit wishes a machine. It wishes the reproduction in humankind of what it is in itself. If people had remained "good" because Spirit had made it impossible to be "bad," then it would not have been real goodness.

We must always remember that humankind is on a long, slow climb upward into the experience of the perfection of God. This ultimate toward which we are traveling is possible only if we are left free to discover our own divinity and to accept it. This is what the whole creative process has been leading up to: the conscious choice of one's "Childship." Unfortunately, humankind from the beginning has made wrong choices. This has been partly due to our acceptance of the reality of a material world apart from Spirit or intelligence. By believing in the reality of the material, we have produced bondage for ourselves.

Little by little, some people have come to realize that the ultimate nature of their own existence is spiritual and not material. Such people have been the great religious geniuses and benefactors of the human race. They are always calling others to understand their essential spiritual nature and to live the life of Spirit here and now. Those who have followed the teaching of these spiritual guides have found that the right choice has brought them freedom in place of bondage. The recognition of their own Childship has opened wide the doors that lead into more satisfying experiences.

Erroneous Materialistic View

Most of us are materialistic because we have spent ages in the worship of the external. We are impressed by the things that we can see, taste, feel, hear and handle. This is one reason that the body commands so much attention. True spiritual philosophy breaks away from this idea of reality of any universe separate from intelligence. It places the body in its rightful place as a created thing and elevates Spirit to its rightful place as supreme in the scheme of life.

Materialists occupy themselves too much with the aches and pains of the body. Searchers for reality look straight through these things to the truth of being. They do not deny that these aches and pains are true in their experience, but they see them as unpleasant images thrown on the screen of their consciousness and then reflected in the physical. Then they proceed through their power of choice to project on that screen the image of perfect health, this health arising not from their will, but from the realization of their own divine inner perfection. Thus they know the imperfect experience to be a false one and the perfect experience to be the only true one in reality.

Money and Reality

In like manner, searchers for reality regard "things," such as money, property, possessions and all sensations connected with them, as belonging to the shadow world of the material. Always they know that the real world of causes is the unseen world within their own consciousness. They admit that "things" are valuable and that it is desirable to pursue them, but they merely hold them; they never allow things to enslave them. Things are never the ultimate reality to searchers of reality. Therefore the loss of these things is never the supreme tragedy. True, it is more pleasant to live in comfort, surrounded by the evidence of prosperity, but ultimate joy is in the giver more than in the gift. Hence, prosperity should be a sign to us that we have contacted the inner reality, and in addition to the material comfort that we enjoy, we rejoice in the inner sense of union with Spirit, which is the cause.

Jesus and Reality

Jesus never belittled the material. He recognized its legitimacy, but he tried constantly to show us that the reality of the material was only a comparative reality and that reality as cause lay much deeper.

Jesus tried to show that "sin" was not so much the performance of certain acts, but more largely in our inner blindness to the hidden eternal that the whole world is unconsciously seeking. "They have eyes to see, but they see not." He tried to show why sorrows come, a sequential effect of concentration on the sense life. He showed that most grief was over the loss of "things" and that the higher people lift their eyes and affections, the less will they experience sorrow. He tried to point the way to the real center of things. He asked that we look straight through the material gold coin to the spiritual idea that formed the coin, so that, having riches within our consciousness, our outer riches would be secure. Without this inner consciousness of oneness with reality, the mere material coin and jewels are liable to rust, to decay or to be stolen.

Jesus' Contact with Reality

One of our problems is that we have thought of Jesus as of different construction from ourselves, and we have lost greatly thereby. Jesus was a person with the same problems to solve that we have. We know that he was possessed of a marvelously complete knowledge of truth; that his was a very complete illumination; that he sensed as perhaps no one before or since has sensed humankind's inseparability from the Divine Presence. But we are inclined to forget that he had to find his way into truth in much the same way that we find ours, because he was not begotten in a different sense than we were. He had to grow into knowledge of truth and his union with God.

Early in life, he saw that there was a far higher plan of living and knowledge than the one on which the majority of people lived. He had the same inner hunger for reality that we have. He was puzzled by the apparent contradictions of life. He probably spent many sleepless nights working on the problem. He saw the treadmill that we call life, in which people were born and lived a certain number of years in sorrow, sickness and disappointment, and he sensed the fact that something was wrong, because surely this could not be *life*. There must be a happier, higher existence, or else the whole scheme of life would be wrong.

Jesus Convinced Himself

During those formative growing years, Jesus must have spent much time trying to adjust his thinking to these new ideas, trying to convince himself that a life of mastery was the real life and could not truly represent reality.

It probably hurt him to see that even his loved ones, who were certainly beautiful people, were blind to this great truth. Perhaps he spent years trying to pierce the veil of the physical, seeing through to the inner spiritual reality, disregarding the appearances of things, knowing the heart of the universe. His family probably opposed his slowly-formulating views, thinking he was "peculiar," if not a lunatic. There may have been long family discussions in which they showed him the "practical" point of view, that of becoming the village carpenter and so making a steady living, forgetting these "harebrained" ideas. Quite possibly, failing as he may have done at times during this spiritual struggle, he may have wondered if the game was worth the candle and whether he should not give up instead of pushing on into the greater, vaster world of spiritual truth that he saw stretching before him.

We must remember that Jesus was not different from us in nature, but he was different in the way he pushed forward into the eternal light. He saw the shadows of life and stepped boldly through them. And when the greatest shadow of all loomed before him, he retired to the garden to prepare himself for the great ordeal. He felt that he needed all the clear vision he could embody so that he could face the crisis.

The Message of Reality

Jesus' message was that humankind was correct in contacting God, the universal principle. The trouble with many people is that they catch glimpses of the possibilities of a larger triumphant life and then hesitate to step forward and go all the way because of the fear of public opinion. It is as though a chick, tired of the cramped life within the shell and with its instinct for life outside urging it on, should stick its head out and then, afraid, withdraw again within the shell. All that beckons us is larger, finer, vastly more satisfying, but it takes courage to go all the way into that life where too few know how to walk.

Practical Aspect of Realization

Jesus plainly taught that the mind of humankind is the place where we use the Mind of God. He held to this truth that there is one power operating through everything. This we also must do. We must realize the supreme intelligence as filling all space and knowing all things, and we must sense that this supreme presence is always clothing itself in temporary form. As far as we are concerned, we must realize that the form it takes for us is the form it takes through our own creative imagination. It stands to reason that the gift of the Spirit must be accepted before it can become realized.

Our Place in the Creative Order

Our place in the creative order is to reproduce in the miniature scale of our individual being the vast creative order of the universe. From this creative power of thought we will never escape; we may merely learn how to use it. If we have been using it destructively and if our use of it has produced lack, fear and physical infirmity, the next logical step to take is to reverse our processes of thought and, no matter what situation we find ourselves in, to realize that God is right there. The law is always available. We must know that we can draw on the divine Presence and Power to meet any and every situation.

Our place in the creative order is to reproduce the cosmos on the plane of the individual, to think God's thoughts after God, and to create our own individual world. If this seems too good to be true, let us stop and ask ourselves the question, "How does anything come into being?" We are certain to be led back to the one, simple, fundamental proposition: The physical universe is the thought of God in form. Our mind is the Mind of God. We are an individualized center of God-consciousness. Hence, our thought is creative, and consequently our world is a product of our thought. Everything then depends on how we think. Our minds are the connecting link between that which we conceive and that which we achieve.

Everything we have today is an extension of the kind of thinking we have been doing. Mind is both omnipresent and omnipotent. If we would lift ourselves out of the treadmill of defeat, we must first start a new activity in Mind. We must identify ourselves with success if we wish to become successful. We must become friendly if we wish to have friends. And we must do this consciously.

We really live in a world of causes, even though it appears that we are living in a world of effects. All causation is spiritual, and all effects are Mind in form. The sickness, defeat, sorrow, want and limitation that we experience are out-picturings of our own thought-life coming into form through inexorable law. If we wish to change these outward forms, we must consciously retreat from the world of effects into the world of causation.

Here we create an entirely new life. Turning our attention from the objective fact to the spiritual reality at the center of our being, fixing our inner vision steadily on the perfection that is, on God the perfect creative principle. And registering here in the universal law a new idea and realizing that this idea must take form, we are complying with the law of our being. We should do this *now*. It is useless to wait until all other people catch this vision. Each one must turn immediately from the darkness of race belief and face the one great light. We must look through the appearance of things as they are to the ultimate reality that can so easily fashion new conditions and mold things as they ought to be.

&

Meditation

I know that in my world I reproduce the creative power of God. In response to my thought, the great creative processes of the universe swing

into action to bring me good or ill in exact correspondence to my beliefs.
Today I turn my thought to positive good. I know that I radiate peace,
love and goodwill, and as a result I draw back to myself peace and love
and goodwill from everyone I meet. I unify myself with material good,
and supply flows to me in the exact measure of my belief. I lift my bowl
of acceptance, and it is now filled to overflowing from the cosmic Horn
of Plenty. Goodness and mercy follow me this day and all the days of my
life, and I dwell contented in the Creator's house.

⌐∕⍭

Questions

1. Have human beings always used their freedom wisely?
2. What is ultimate reality?
3. Why must the gift of the Spirit be accepted before it is realized?
4. Do all people use the creative power of thought?
5. What is our place in the creative order?

Answers

1. We each have the power of choice and freedom of will. We have made wrong choices because we have believed in the ultimate reality of a material world and so have used our freedom unwisely.
2. Ultimate reality is necessarily Spirit. From this Spirit flows what is called "the material universe," the body of God.
3. The gift of the Spirit must be accepted before it is realized, because we must have a concept of any gift before it can be manifested.
4. All people use the creative power of thought. We use it every time we think. Unfortunately we too frequently use it destructively.
5. Our place in the creative order is to establish a cosmos in our individual experience or microcosm, as God does in the macrocosm.

Improving Material Conditions

✑

Students of the Science of Mind should develop a well-balanced outlook on life. The very nature of the study that we are undertaking brings us face to face with the most dynamic law humankind has ever discovered. For perhaps the first time, we are truly sensing the tremendous possibility of a life lived in the clear light of reason. For the first time, we are being made aware of potentialities that are far beyond the experience of the average person.

Naturally when one affirms that the universe in which we are living is a spiritual system governed by the laws of thought, those who have given only a little thought to the subject may think they are announcing that one can have whatever one wants, can do exactly as one sees fit, and can dominate and control everything within one's reach. Fortunately, however, this is only partly true. There is nothing either unreasonable or irrational about this Science. It is intensely sane, practical and never should be connected with anything weird or outrageous.

Therefore, if anyone asks you, "Can I become a millionaire overnight simply by affirming that I have a million dollars?" your answer would be that nothing could be further from the truth. There are too many misguided people in dire circumstances who are affirming "I am rich." In a certain sense their affirmation is correct, but frequently they overlook the fundamental premise of the Science of Mind, which is that the Spirit can do for us only that which it does *through* us. Too often people make the mistake of mentally wishing instead of intelligently thinking. Too often they fail to realize that they have a definite part to play in the relationship between God and themselves.

Intelligent Thought Improves Conditions

It is unquestionably true that Science of Mind, properly understood and applied, can and does improve one's material conditions. It is likewise true that those who clearly know their oneness with all supply will incorporate that affirmation into their personal science of living. But Science of Mind is certainly not a get-rich-quick scheme that enables one to ignore the laws of the universe and simply affirm oneself into wealth. We receive more as we grow more, and as we grow, we learn more perfectly to apply those principles that underlie all successful action. Proper understanding of this relationship to the universe, backed up by intelligent, industrious work, will add materially to our measure of success. Work without vision is drudgery, but vision without work is self-deception. Well-balanced individuals are those who can walk with their heads in the clouds and still keep their feet solidly planted on the ground. Faith and work are conjoined twins that die when separated.

We Cannot Go Against Law

Those who wish to demonstrate happiness will never be able to do so while their consciousness remains filled with thoughts of disharmony. If they give over the major portion of their waking hours to dwelling on thoughts of unhappiness, of the injustice of others toward them, of their unlovable qualities, of the hard row they have to hoe compared with that of others, then they might just as well give up the illusion that they will ever experience peace. But the very moment they deliberately cast out every thought of self-pity and consciously turn away from the apparent injustices of life, then they have started on their demonstration of happiness.

Demonstrating Supply

In like manner, we cannot spend our time saturating our consciousness with thoughts of limitation and expect to manifest prosperity. It may be true that the bills are not paid and work may be scarce, but in Science of Mind we must learn that the very first step toward right action lies in *knowing*, and if we are to change our outward condition, we must first change our inner contemplation. Even when we are explaining to the collector at the door just why we cannot meet that bill today, we must learn to detach ourselves from the acceptance of poverty as a normal state, or even a reasonable one. This does not mean that we vainly dismiss our obligation to others with a wave of our hand. We recognize its validity, but at the same time we know that our present straitened circumstances are the ultimate result of past years of a poverty consciousness, a "times are tough" consciousness, and we determine that our coming years will be colored by the opposite consciousness.

Difficult to change? Yes, particularly after a lifetime of thinking. But when we are definitely changing from the average person's thought and making up our mind to go against the stream of average thinking, we know that we must expect to exert a special effort at first in changing the entire life-current of our thought. The rewards will repay us, because we will move out of that old set of circumstances as surely as the sun rises. As surely as the inner attitude changes, the outer will change in conformity to it, quickly or slowly, according to the measure of the mental acceptance.

Freedom Is the Law of Spirit

If the thought arises that maybe all people are not intended to know this freedom from financial worries, that perhaps there is some unrevealed reason why an inscrutable Providence allows us to continue in hardship, then let us remember that it is always the purpose of life to increase that which we have rather than to take it away. An argument from nature may help us at this point.

Nature always spurs on every living thing to greater freedom and renders us intolerant of anything which hampers that freedom. The bird trapped in the forest and placed in a cage will often soon die in its frantic efforts to escape and enjoy its freedom. This is an inner urge that is entirely unreasoned. It is the urge of ever-expanding Spirit. The wild animal paces incessantly up and down, seeking a way of escape from the limiting cage. Tree roots will break through a sidewalk for freedom. The prisoner braves death in the swift currents of the bay and the shark-infested waters to gain freedom. People fight for freedom until exterminated. The will toward freedom is an instinct in everything that lives.

It may be freedom from an individual or freedom from poverty or from criticism or from the absence of love, but whatever the reason, it is still an urge for freedom, even though it may be mistaken. So is the urge for a nicer home, a better automobile, more sales, a bigger paycheck or a more important job. It is not necessarily a reasoned impulse. It may not even be recognized, and certainly not premeditated. It is inherent in the law of our being. We cannot deny it and be happy.

Spiritual Basis for Material Increase

It is not a sign of greed when one desires to build a bigger business or earn a larger paycheck. This is a natural urge, because it is the endeavor of Spirit to multiply its gifts to us so that it may multiply its self-expression through us. It is its nature to express freedom, because greater freedom for us means greater expression of the life that is the Creator of us all.

When Is Freedom Wrong?

The only time freedom is wrong for us is when it infringes on the freedom of another. Our freedom ends where the other person's freedom begins. Since we can only get what we get through the operation of the law, then that same law is the law of freedom for our neighbor as well as for ourselves.

Dishonesty, fraud or deliberate infliction of suffering on others can never be connected with our getting what we want. If the thing we want will hurt another, then we have misused the law

This should not be misconstrued to mean that we will never hurt anyone by our decisions. Sometimes other people seek to keep us from obtaining our freedom with the plaint that, by so doing, we will make them unhappy. As a matter of fact, they are infringing on our freedom every day that they keep us in bondage.

Many people today are remaining in bondage and stifling the free flow of Spirit through them by remaining in a situation that is a barrier to their growth, simply because they are told that by leaving it, they would rob another selfish person of happiness. Sometimes these are parents who hold their unmarried children by pleading with them not to leave home in order to better themselves or by asking them not to marry because "I would be so lonely." This is a crass selfishness on the part of people who have lived their lives fully and who now would deny their children natural expression in a normal fulfillment.

Children therefore have to make their own decision about this question, and the pleading of the parents tends to stifle the real facts in the case. Few are willing to appear hard-hearted toward a parent, so they decide to remain in bondage. What such people should see clearly is that the unhappiness is not caused by their selfishness, but by the other's selfishness that would hold them in violation of universal law. It is like the child who, reproved for pulling the cat's tail, replies, "I was not pulling it; I was only holding it. The cat was doing the pulling."

Seeing Ourselves in Perfection

We have spoken frequently of the necessity of turning completely away from undesirable conditions and forming new thought habits by an active choice or selection of the opposite condition. We should take time daily to see ourselves as we really want to be. We should see ourselves as living happily in our new circumstances, then bringing into our contemplation the particular event in which our happiness seems to center. It may be a happy marriage, a new home, a business of our own or a better business, but whatever it is, there should be a quiet, unstrained acceptance of the fact that *it is right for us, is possible for us, and is ours already in Mind*. We should keep ourselves wide open to it, completely receptive to it, and should surround it with a real warmth of loving expectation. We should regard it joyously, knowing that it will increase our happiness and never diminish it.

Subjective States Bring Conditions

We should never lose sight of the fact that it is our subjective mental state that produces our outward conditions. This is fundamental, and no matter how often repeated throughout this book, it is never redundant. It is always necessary. True, other factors enter in, such as our willingness to work industriously, carefully saving instead of wasting money and doing the very best work of which we are capable, whether we work for others or are in business for ourselves. But the determining factor, first and last, is our own subjective state, which as a result of our study we now realize can be changed. We have the power within our own thought to remold old patterns into new conditions.

Approach the Law Naturally

We must rid ourselves of any tendency toward superstition regarding the law. The vast expanse of Universal Mind receives our thought just as impersonally as the ocean receives the drop of water during a rain and makes that drop what it is itself. Mind does this with our "thought-drops." They may seem insignificant and puerile to us, but to Mind they are received and incorporated into itself. Thus Mind starts to carry our thought forward into demonstration. In its impersonalness, the law of Mind takes every individual thought and turns it into outward conditions, good or bad. This great universal ocean of Mind, which we call the law, is what might be termed *the impersonal side of God* and should be approached as normally and naturally as we would approach the soil when planting seed, knowing that it will receive any seed from anybody and grow it into manifestation.

The Impersonal Side of God

The impersonal side of God means the law of Mind, or the law of cause and effect. We have already discussed the thought that God as pure Spirit is personal to each one of us, although the universe as a law of cause and effect is always impersonal. While it is true that this concept of the personal and the impersonal aspects of the universe can easily lead to intellectual confusion, it is equally true that this true understanding of the nature of reality is perhaps the most important plank in the whole platform of the Science of Mind.

Every law of nature that we know anything about is subject to conscious use as far as we are concerned. The laws of nature, being impersonal, do not know who is using them or for what purpose. Nor does the law have any personal choice in the matter. Its nature always is to obey. When we speak of the impersonal side of God, we are really referring to the whole universe of law, whether we call such laws physical or metaphysical.

The personal side of God, that is, the spiritual essence of reality, is the divine intelligence with which we commune through intuition and by meditation, bringing us into a conscious and direct relationship with the Parent Mind. This has always been the office of prayer and of spiritual contemplation, and it is necessary that the student of this Science should spend definite time in this inner communion with the Over-Soul. It is this Over-Soul that is our over- or universal-self. However, when it comes to using the laws of nature, we are no longer seeking direct communion with Spirit. Rather, we are acting in accord with the inspiration that we have drawn from Spirit. We are dealing with the impersonal side of the universe. We are dealing with a government of law. How can we expect this law to do anything for us in a definite way unless we first consciously understand how the law works and as consciously use it for definite purposes? This is what constitutes the technique of any science.

Unfortunately, many people seem to think that when they approach the Science of Mind they are no longer dealing with definite laws of cause and effect. For some peculiar reason they feel that they are entering a new field of causation where law no longer controls. But such is not the case. The laws of Mind are just as exacting as other laws. It is impossible for the mental law with which we deal to know anything about us as individuals that we fail to recognize about ourselves. We might say that the law of Mind has no specific intention whatsoever relative to the individual life until the individual gives it such intention. But once having received this intention that the individual imparts to it, the very fact that it is subjective and impersonal makes it necessary for the law to respond *by correspondence*. In this way, when we pass an idea over to Mind, it at once begins to act creatively on it without argument, without delay and without deviating one iota from the concept that we hand to it. This will explain one of the great mysteries that the great teachers of the ages have announced, but which few people have properly analyzed. For instance, Jesus told us that when we ask God for anything, we must believe that we already have the thing we are asking for. This is a veiled statement of the law of cause and effect. It really means that we must have a mental acceptance of our desire before the law can act on that desire in an affirmative way.

That is why in this Science when we give mental treatments, we are told to accept the thing we desire even before we experience it, because unless we accept it, we are rejecting it, and if we are rejecting it we are not believing that we have it, and while we believe that we do not have it, the law cannot make the gift. Hence, we are told to believe that we already possess the object of our desire and so should make known our requests with thanksgiving. A little thought given to this matter will clearly demonstrate that there is no other way prayer could be answered and there is no other way demonstration could be made. We have the inspiration, intuition, the instruction of the illumined, the dictates of common sense and a definite knowledge of the law of cause and effect and how it works in practical experience. From all these sources we draw this one and inevitable conclusion. When a mental treatment is given, it must incorporate the affirmative acceptance of the object of its desire. It must state that it now *already has* what it desires, and it must accept a complete fulfillment.

❧

Meditation

I am endowed with absolute control over my thinking. I know that my thoughts are productive and do produce actual experiences in my life. I have no fear of lack or limitation in any form, because I know God's plan is abundance. That abundance is my supply. I cannot be deprived of God's supply. No person, place or thing can interfere with the flow of Divine Substance manifesting in my life as my own wealth. Omnipresent substance is everywhere, evenly present. It is the source of everything that is. The source of this substance is my source, and I am now directing my thought only to that source. I see myself receiving all the supply I will ever need or want. I identify myself with this supply and give thanks for it.

⌒⌒

Questions

1. Why must we turn away from negative thoughts?
2. What is the meaning of the expression "Freedom is the law of Spirit"?
3. Is our freedom ever curtailed?
4. Explain the idea that subjective mind is impersonal.
5. Why should we believe that we already have the thing for which we have asked?

Answers

1. Since thought is always creative, to entertain negative thinking is to invite unsatisfactory and limiting experiences. Thus we turn away from negative thoughts.
2. It is the nature of Spirit to express freedom. Greater freedom for us means more complete expression for Spirit.
3. Our freedom is never curtailed except when it conflicts with another's freedom.
4 Subjective mind is law, and all law is impersonal. It receives the impress of thought and acts on it spontaneously and without argument.
5. We believe in an impersonal law that is at once creative and intelligent. It must respond to us by corresponding to our thought. A belief that we *already have* automatically starts a tendency in the law to produce the corresponding effect.

Hindrance to Healing

Many people who can answer all the questions asked about the mechanics of the healing process fail to receive help because they are unwilling to pay the price. This price often involves the giving up of some pet weakness or of some pet emotional or mental mood, and it usually involves the cultivation of some positive attitude.

When Jesus said, "Go, sin no more lest a worse thing come upon you," he was not threatening or using an appeal to fear. Sin means making a mistake or missing the mark. There is no sin except a mistake and no punishment except a consequence. So when Jesus said, "Go, sin no more," he was not hurling theological invective; he was merely pointing to the law of cause and effect.

It stands to reason that if certain mental attitudes have produced certain conditions, then a continuation of such attitudes will perpetuate such conditions. There must always be soul-searching to find whether or not we are living in accord with the law of harmony. One thing is certain, we cannot fool the universe. This is what true spiritual analysis does for the mind. It sets it back on the right track, always pointing to the great reality that harmoniously governs everything.

Healing Comes from Unity

Once we have grasped the idea that healing follows in such degree as we have realized our oneness with God, we are very likely to ask, "Just how far does this oneness with God extend?" The answer is, "It extends just as far as you allow it." When we understand this oneness, we can realize that the more closely our thoughts and actions coincide with the divine nature, the more perfectly we reproduce God, and the more perfectly we reproduce God, the more effectively we will control God's creative law. Thus, as we open our lives to the inflow of divine healing power, we release everything God-like *through* us.

Necessity for Love

Just as we should recognize our oneness with the All-Health, so should we recognize our oneness with the All-Love. There is only one health in the entire universe, and we enjoy this when we associate ourselves intimately with it. There is only one love in the universe, and we receive it by associating ourselves with it. Since there is only one Mind in the entire universe, we receive it by associating ourselves with it. This Mind is the Mind of God, full of life and intelligence for all. This life is overflowing with healing love. Therefore, as we become one with it, we enter into the experience of that which is unsick, untroubled and at peace.

No Room for Hatred

As we enter into oneness with the All-Love, we will find less and less room for hatred, bitterness, criticism and envy. We will open our inner lives to the perfect, free, unhindered inflow of divine love. Thus we pass from an experience (healing) into a life (knowing God). We raise our life to a higher level, a level where there is a consuming de-

178

sire to do good to others and where lower desires gradually fade out. We will give no room to personal enmities. If there have been enemies, we freely forgive them, because hatred and healing can never abide in the same consciousness, nor in the same body.

It is at this very point where many healings break down. We want our "blessings," but we want to retain a pet bitterness toward someone else. In a sense, this retention of a bitter feeling is a subjective desire to shut others off from a blessing similar to that which we have received, and in thus mentally shutting them off, we unknowingly shut ourselves off.

Those who hold grudges break away from the highest use of their divine consciousness. God never hates, nor does God hold feelings of bitterness toward any person. Thus the grudge-holder is trying to express God and something else, which is impossible. God is not cut-up into little sections. No one can say, "I will express God's healing, but not God's love." Since God is indivisible, those who refrain from expressing their love find themselves unable to express their health. Therefore, we should express love, because love is the fulfilling of the law.

We Forgive Right Now

Those who are spiritually aware of their oneness with God freely forgive everyone with whom they have ever had a difference. They do not wait until they feel themselves to be in a forgiving mood. They do not even wait to separate the sheep from the goats and say, "These I can freely forgive, but these others are too mean, so I'll reserve a little private hatred for them." No, we take them all into the arms of love at once without waiting to ask if they are deserving or not. Here is a good affirmation to use in this regard: "I bless and love everything that God has created. God sees God's self in God's handiwork, and so do I. I refuse to see anything ugly in anyone. I now look for and find the good in all people, even those who hurt me."

This does not mean that we must accept everyone's opinion

about us or that we must agree with those ideas that we feel are contradictory to an intelligent outlook on life. It merely means that we maintain a good-natured flexibility in our relationship with people. In spiritual mind treatment, it means that we must separate our thought about the real person from our thought about what ails the physical or psychological person. The real person is always spiritual and perfect. It is the psychological and physiological person who needs to be healed.

We may have sympathy with people without sympathizing with their troubles. We can enter into a consciousness of love for another's spiritual nature without entering into a consciousness of unity with either their psychological or physiological discord. For instance, if you are treating clients who have had a great deal of discord or hate in their lives, you must rise above both their psychological reactions to life and their physiological correspondents. You must cause your own consciousness to rise in love and appreciation for their real natures to a place where your love has consumed all of the hate and, by its very presence, has destroyed all other discord. Any denials and affirmations that you make in this upward mental path toward your spiritual goal, which is a true appreciation of humankind's real nature, are for the purpose of clarifying your own thought and removing any obstructions from it that deny you the right to rise above the discord and the confusion to the place where your affirmation becomes a more complete announcement of the divine harmony.

Sin and Punishment

From the foregoing, one can readily see that it is not a matter of a personal God withdrawing favors from a stubborn child who refuses to cooperate. There is no such thing as punishment for sin. We are punished *by* our sins, never *for* them. Every action, every thought that we think, carries within itself its own consequence for good or ill. Every act is tied inseparably to its own consequence, and we can no more get away from the consequences of our thoughts than we can get away from our own shadow. It has been truly said that the spiritual confessional is the greatest psychiatrist on earth. Jesus sometimes forgave people their sins before he administered the healing word. Some psychologists tell us that there is a secret sense of guilt behind all neurosis. If so, how important it is that the mental practitioner remove the pressure of this burden on the psychic life.

It is a correct use of this Science to realize that God holds nothing against anyone and that the divine forgivingness is a necessary complement to the divine givingness. Any sense of guilt that we have, any burden of condemnation that we entertain or any mental state that weights us down hinders us from demonstrating the eternal goodness. Mental practitioners remove these obstructions. We explain to our clients that sin is a result of ignorance. We enlighten them by showing them that the Spirit never holds anything against them, but we also very carefully explain that since the law of cause and effect is always working, punishment will always follow wrong doing. It would be impossible for us to undergo a series of spiritual mind treatments without arriving at a more clarified spiritual position in our own thought. We not only would be less likely to make mistakes, but we would have less desire to engage in any destructive act or thought.

What about Medical Assistance?

Some schools of metaphysics believe that it is wrong to seek medical or pharmaceutical assistance under any circumstances. While we hold no controversy over this subject, it is entirely fitting that we make our position clear. The Science of Mind has no superstitions, holds to no formulas, and believes in the good in everything. We sincerely believe that any physical condition can be changed through the proper use of prayer, faith or spiritual affirmation. We are equally certain that not all people who have asked for help have finally been healed. If one is able to say to a paralyzed person, "Take up your bed and walk" and have the person immediately proceed to actually take up their bed and walk, then there is certainly no point left to argue over. What right have we to deny anyone whatever help they can find?

Possibly someone will say, "But are you not resorting to material means in order to assist the Spirit?" The answer is, "Not at all." There are no material means as far as Spirit is concerned. Divine Intelligence has conceived and created everything, and everything that God has made must be good if we could only understand its true nature. The mental attitude that one cannot receive spiritual benefit if one is being attended by a physician seems to us to be built on superstition. Rather, we believe in the most complete cooperation among all of the healing arts, as we also believe in the most complete cooperation between the physician, the metaphysician, the psychological and the spiritual counselor.

We know that the highest form of mental healing is spiritual healing. This spiritual healing may be a result of earnest prayer or exalted faith or of spiritual affirmations. It is useless to quibble over terms. We know that faith and conviction must be arrived at. It does not seem fruitful to argue over what methods one should use or to say, or that one method is right while another is wrong. Any method that is constructive is right if it finally arrives at the desired goal. Why not combine them all and thereby happily arrive at the greatest good that is possible at our present state of evolution?

As previously pointed out, the fact that all branches of the healing profession succeed in healing is an indication that underneath all these healings there must be some contact with a hidden healing principle that is universal. As one wise physician said, "I treat the patient, but God does the healing." Practitioners who understand this principle do their work steadily holding in Mind that the client is divinely perfect, that the manifestation of disease is in reality no part of the real person, and that the client's body is pure spiritual substance. We work with these ideas until we convince ourselves that our client is a spiritual entity living in a perfect existence, divinely guided, controlled and maintained.

More often than not, our clients are not able to follow this idea. But though they haven't thought the proposition out, they will receive benefit just the same. As far as the treatment is concerned, it begins and ends in the mind of the one giving it. Just how it reaches the client, no one knows, nor is it necessary to try to find out. We know that we do not hold thoughts for our clients. We do not suggest anything to them, and we do not will anything for them. What we try to do is to recognize their spiritual nature, to realize the divine presence of perfection in, around and through them, functioning in every organ of their being. Practitioners work with these ideas until, in their own minds, they realize the truth about their clients. This is all that we could do, this is all that we need try to do, and if we do this successfully, our work will be effective.

The Practitioner Holds Life

It is a serious thing to accept the responsibility of treating the sick, because in a sense practitioners hold the life of the client in their hands. We should constantly keep ourselves alive to the greatness of the power with which we deal, its instant availability, its irresistibility and its thoroughness and intelligence. We should spend much time in meditation on our oneness with the Divine Presence and in the contemplation of the fact that all people, no matter how apparently ill, are indivisibly one with this same Presence. And never for one moment should we allow ourselves to admit even secretly that some diseases are amenable to treatment while others are not. We must persistently *know* without the slightest equivocation that everyone who comes to us for treatment can be helped, no matter what their physical condition may be.

∽

Meditation

Indwelling me are all the qualities and attributes that I will ever need or want. The Spirit within me is the Infinite Presence. I am life. I live in this Presence. I am love. I enjoy the love of my community, and I am responding by expressing love toward all life. I am intelligence. All knowing is established within me. I use this intelligence when I think, act and do. It is limitless. Therefore I instantly know everything I need. I express intelligence, wisdom and knowledge. I am power. I have strength and limitless endurance. I can accomplish anything that I am called on to do. Because God works in me, I cannot fail. I am now radiant with life, love intelligence, substance and power. I believe in my own spiritual self and its ability to act as me. I believe in my own soul, and I respond fearlessly to its prompting. I am willing to let go and accept the privilege of radiating my true self. From this moment forth, I intend to live in the source of my being. My thought is concentrated on my oneness in God.

Questions

1. Can those who harbor enmity in their minds be good practitioners?
2. How soon should we forgive the those who have done us a wrong?
3. Are we punished for wrong thinking?
4. What is the attitude of the student of Science of Mind toward doctors and medicine?
5. Of what do practitioners try to convince themselves?

Answers

1. It is necessary to always have a forgiving spirit. Those who harbor hatred in their hearts cannot be good practitioners.
2. Forgiveness should follow immediately on the recognition of a wrong done to another. We cultivate the spirit of forgiveness, which has no room for hate.
3. We are not punished for wrong thinking, but we must suffer the consequence of it.

4. In the Science of Mind philosophy, we seek help from anyone who can give it. We do not believe that enlisting the services of a physician prevents us from attaining spiritual healing. We believe that the mental causation that brought trouble must be changed in order that there may be no reappearance of the difficulty.

5. Practitioners try to convince themselves of the perfection of their clients.

Do We Deny Human Suffering?

⌘

We most certainly do not deny human suffering, which in some form or other seems to come upon everyone. What we affirm is that suffering is an experience, rather than a thing in itself. Naturally, we all have had more of this experience than we desire, and from a common sense viewpoint, we could hardly expect anyone to go through life without meeting this problem. We should therefore find out how best to adapt ourselves to unpleasant occurrences in order that they may do us the least harm and that we may get the most good from them.

We cannot believe that suffering is a part of the divine plan, because this would be philosophically unsound. If we have a suffering first cause, then the entire universe must eternally suffer with it. This of course would be a house divided against itself and is both absurd and unthinkable. In some manner that we do not completely understand, we feel that all suffering is a result of ignorance, and we know that the only thing that heals ignorance is knowledge. Knowledge alone gives power.

The Outer and the Inner

There are two ways of looking at everything. There is an outer and an inner meaning to all life. Carl Jung, in his book *Psychology and Religion*, tells us that it is impossible to account for anything visible without first understanding that it must have an invisible cause. It stands to reason that every effect must have a cause. If we are starting with the supposition that the universe is a spiritual system governed by laws of thought, then it follows that discordant thought will produce discordant conditions. The outer will always be a reflection of the inner.

A wise person once said that we will be subject to suffering as long as we inflict pain on others. This seems like sound philosophy. It is certainly good logic, and it does keep faith with the reasonableness of cause and effect. It is one thing to acknowledge that we have undergone suffering; it is quite another thing to believe that this suffering is imposed on us by some external force, intelligence or will. If, on the other hand, we can come to the conclusion that suffering is a result of an ignorant use of the law of cause and effect, then in ascertaining its cause we will also discover its cure. We get right back to the old, simple but profound proposition that every problem carries its own answer with it.

Generally speaking, whenever the medical profession discovers the cause of any disease, it knows how to successfully deal with it. When we discover the hidden mental cause for any particular form of suffering, why shouldn't we then consciously change this cause and, as a logical result of having changed it, reverse its effect? In doing this we would not be destroying the law of cause and effect itself; we would merely be using it in a different way. In our philosophy, we follow this rule as completely as possible, and we say something to this effect: If a sense of always having one's feelings hurt can produce certain inflammation in the throat area, which experience seems to verify, then why would it not follow that if we arrived at a place where our feelings were no longer hurt, the physical correspondent would also disappear?

We would add one more thought to this, which is that as long as we give cause to others for having their feelings hurt, we ourselves are subject to a like sequence of cause and effect. This places the whole problem where it belongs, because no problem can be solved that is external to consciousness. If we assume causes for human suffering beyond our reach, then they are beyond the possibility of change. If, on the other hand, we assume that the hidden cause of our negative experience must be within the realm of our conscious control, then we are not bound by any law of suffering; we are merely bound by a misunderstanding of the way the law of cause and effect operates.

Jesus understood this perfectly when he forgave people their sins, and we have one instance in particular that was outstanding in his experience and teaching. When they brought the blind man to Jesus and asked, "Who did sin? Who made the mistake? This man or his parents?" Jesus did not argue the problem with them. He took the position that no matter what caused the man's blindness, it could be reversed. In our work, we must always take the position that truth overcomes every apparent obstruction, that we may consciously use the hidden cause to change any manifest effect. We do not believe that there is any cosmic purpose in suffering or that the universe is imposing great lessons on us through suffering. We believe that ignorance alone is its cause, and enlightenment alone will heal it. This is not only a sensible attitude, it is equally a scientific one.

Cause and Effect

There are many sufferings that our reason can justify, so these do not cause us mental distress. For instance, the ache that follows when one eats green apples, or such things as broken down nerves or a weakened digestive system following indulgence in destructive thoughts such as worry, anger, etc. There is another suffering that is harder to reconcile: the agony through which beautiful souls are sometimes compelled to pass. We answer these problems by saying that we are all more or less subject to the entire race belief and that each one of us is more or less bound by the sum total of human thought until we individually free ourselves. This is a solid position to take and is supported by both reason and certain psychological factors that, more and more, are coming to be recognized in the field of mental science.

From a practical viewpoint, the student of the Science of Mind views any and all suffering as a logical outcome of hidden causes. In seeking a relief from suffering, we deliberately reverse these causes and therefore heal their effects. We do not deal with the effect; we deal with the cause, destroying it at its roots and permitting its effect to dry up for lack of nourishment. In actual practice, those using this Science theoretically resolve things into thoughts, taking the position that wherever any circumstance or experience denies the fundamental harmony, it is basically wrong. It is built on the belief in a suppositional opposite to good. Practitioners declare that good is the only cause, and knowing that suffering is a result of a false use of this cause, we build up a consciousness that contradicts the belief in the necessity of suffering, which affirms the presence of the desired experience rather than the undesirable one. This rule will prove to be effective in any and all mental treatments.

Pain as Friend and Teacher

Physical pain is really not an enemy, since it calls attention to serious conditions that need to be changed, thus enabling us to take the proper steps in rearranging our lives. Therefore, we should not be bitter over suffering nor become melancholy through having experienced it. To do this would be to lose the lesson entirely. On the other hand, we must be equally certain that we do not fall under the mistaken idea that the suffering is imposed on us by some deific power, as though God were tantalizing us or clubbing us into acquiescence to the divine will. All experiences should tend to develop the real purpose of life, which is to arrive at an understanding of the divine center within us.

Evil is not a problem in itself, and yet evil is more than a belief. Limitation is more than imagination, and we cannot consider physical pain or want as being illusion. Quite naturally, the primitive religions taught a dualistic view of the universe. There were two hostile powers: God and the devil, or good and evil forever locked in a struggle for our souls. We can trace this belief through our own Christian theology, through that of the Hebrews, Persians and Babylonians. But merely because millions of people have believed in the necessity of evil or that evil is imposed on us by some outside source, we need not accept this verdict. The fact that many people believe a thing to be true will not necessarily make it so. We view all evil, lack, want, limitation, sickness, pain and human suffering as a negation of truth, actual enough as an experience, but nevertheless a denial of the life principle itself.

There is only one way for us to prove that this is a correct position, and that is to put our philosophy to the test of actual experience. Suppose, for instance, you are suffering from a lack of friendship. You have no friends, see no friends, believe in no friends, and therefore you are isolated from the great stream of consciousness that makes up humanity. It might be a little difficult at first to show you that the cause is in your own subconscious belief. As a matter of fact, it wouldn't heal you merely to tell you this. You must be taught to reverse your processes of thought relative to friendship. You must be taught to become friendly. In actual practice, you are taught mentally to see friends everywhere you go, to believe that everyone you meet will be friendly, to expect happy human relationships. You must go even further than this and make the definite declaration that friendship is the law of your life. This law is a law of the universe now being enforced in your own individual experience. Gradually, as you reverse your inner thought processes, you will find a change coming in your external world. People will become friendly. You will be invited to group gatherings, others will include you in their community thought, and finally you will discover yourself to be a center through which love and friendship flow out and come back again into your own experience.

Our ideas of good and evil are more or less relative. As we awaken to the consciousness that certain things do not work out well, we seek a greater good and call the lesser good *evil*. In the dim ages of antiquity, our ancestors lived by the law of strength. They killed each other without any qualms of conscience. But slowly, as the human race evolved, people became dimly aware of stirrings within them that proclaimed their divinity, and gradually a new standard was established. Personal killings became murder, taking what belonged to another became theft, etc. Until that time, there was no consciousness of sin, because humankind was complying with the law of its lower self. Having no consciousness of sin, people had no sense of guilt. But the more perfect standard emerged as we pushed upward from the lower levels of living and time made "ancient good uncouth."

If we were to carry this proposition to its ultimate conclusion, we should see that somewhere along the line of our evolution, we will arrive at a place where it will be impossible for us to wish harm to others. When that time comes, it will be equally impossible for harm to be imposed on us. This new vision is not so much a theological mandate or a philosophical conception as it is a matter of awakening to the greater good. It is something that comes from the stirrings of the Divine Spirit within us.

In the new psychological outlook on alcoholism, for instance, patients are not taught so much to resist the desire as they are taught to envision a new life in which this desire to drink plays no important part whatsoever. The habit thus dies for lack of nourishment. In mental practice, practitioners dealing with such cases work to know that their Spirit, being some part of the Spirit of God, is entirely free from any or all vicious desires. They are happy and satisfied within themselves. They find a natural stimulant in their contemplation of Spirit, and a logical outlet for the urge toward self-expression is found in constructive action. The energies of the old habits are transmuted through the alchemy of spiritual understanding into a new form of self-expression. This new self-expression is so much more complete than the old that it entirely obliterates it. The old habit has not been driven out; it has merely ceased to function. This is a very good example of how it is that our work is not so much will as it is willingness. It is never mental coercion or compulsion. It is rather a release of the higher faculties within us. It is really the uncovering of a more divine standard. Goodness and badness as entities do not enter into this, but are merely different levels of experience, and the expanding soul always has a tendency to choose the higher level.

We believe that behind all these processes of thought is an actual reality in the universe that, properly adhered to, causes everything to work out rightly. When in ignorance of our true nature we violate it, the reaction of the law must of necessity be a violent one. The attendant experience of pain, lack or disharmony warns us that we are on the wrong track, and we begin to inquire why. For every problem that confronts us, we set up a "why" and are never satisfied until the problem is solved. Somehow or other we instinctively know that we are born to be free. Thus Moses said that God sets before us a blessing and a curse. It is a blessing if you obey the commandments, a curse if you disobey them.

Whenever we go contrary to the harmonious laws of our being, we suffer. Whenever we live in accord with harmony, we are automatically released from suffering. The pleasure-pain principle of psychology, which we believe has a great deal of merit, is an automatic provision of nature, destined finally to lead us to that place in consciousness where it will be impossible to desire pain for ourselves or others. When this place will have been reached, suffering will automatically cease. This swings us back to the fundamental proposition on which our entire system of thought is built: *There is one power in the universe, but there are two ways of using it.*

We seem to have two general methods for arriving at the proper use of the life principle. One way, we call intuition; the other we call experience. Fortunately or unfortunately, most of us learn through experience. Perhaps as our evolution progresses, our conscious contact with reality will become so deepened that much painful experience will be eliminated. There seems to be no time-set for this devoutly-to-be-longed-for consummation to take place. In all probability, we set the time ourselves. One thing is certain: While we would give pain, we will receive it; while we would be the cause of hurt, we may become hurt.

The universe itself is foolproof, and somewhere along the line each one of us will have to learn that love is the only all-conquerable principle of nature—a love so limitless, deep and broad that people have renamed it *God*. Suppose we start then with the proposition that the universe itself desires only our good, that fundamentally it is for us and never against us. And suppose we add to this proposition the idea that what the creative principle does for us, it must do *through* us. Will we not, of necessity, arrive at the conclusion that our whole processes of thought should be changed to comply with this new mental outlook? Generally speaking, this change of thought, this conversation of consciousness is not brought about in a moment's time. It does not follow, however, that since it is not brought about in a moment's time that life should resolve itself into a continual struggle. Suppose we take the happier mental outlook and become willing to gradually change our mental outlook. In actual practice we should take a few moments every day to mentally realize our freedom and to sense spiritually that we are surrounded by an eternal goodness, and in our imagination we should picture our lives as more nearly ideal.

After we have set this mental scene, we should declare that this new vision is now the law unto our experience. We should affirm that we are surrounded by an infinite intelligence that directs us and an infinite power that propels us and an infinite goodness whose whole desire is that we will experience a complete livingness, a perfect joy. As we set this mental stage, we should also realize that we must become the actor on it. We must inwardly think and outwardly act as though the ideal were the real. At first this may be difficult, but as we more and more become rewarded through the action of the law of cause and effect, which brings greater good into our experience, we will more completely come to see that we are dealing with an absolute and immutable law, and we will no longer set any limit to the good that we are to experience. Having realized what good is, we will now seek to embody it. We will enter into the greatest partnership in life: the partnership of our soul with the Oversoul. In the close intimacy of this conscious interior contact with reality, we will come to sense a divine presence overshadowing and indwelling us. We will not become less in this presence. Quite the reverse. In it we will find our real selves.

∽

Meditation

I know that the divine urge within me is expressing through me as desire. All great things come through recognition. I am now directing my desires to recognize and accept the reality of love, harmony, intelligence and substance. My thought is constantly molding the realities of the invisible into conditions and environments of my objective world. I am now shaping my desires into the mold I wish to have as an actual experience in my life. I recognize that the desire to express health is the activity of God-life in every cell of my being. In this instant, I erase all fear of physical or mental imperfection. I am free. I recognize lavish abundance manifesting all around me. Therefore, I no longer entertain thoughts of lack. My supply comes to me from every direction. I recognize harmony and order. I see it everywhere. I do not associate my thinking with confusion of any kind. I am never unbalanced or disturbed in any way. All things work together for good, and that good is mine now.

∽

Questions

1. What do we believe to be the cause of suffering?
2. Explain the idea of "The outer will always be a reflection of the inner."

3. How is it possible to realize desired effects?
4. Explain the expression, "Our work is not so much will as it is willingness."
5. What are the two ways of arriving at reality?

Answers

1. All suffering is the result of ignorance, ignorance of the law of cause and effect.
2. Since the universe is a spiritual system governed by laws of thought, then thought (cause) must precede manifestation (effect). Thought (inner) produces an effect (outer), which is its equivalent.
3. We can secure effects by reversing causation, by putting new spiritual causation in motion.
3. Our work is never coercion. It is never compulsion or effect of the will. We open channels (intelligence) for divine influx.
5. We arrive at reality by intuition and through objective experience.

THE SCOPE AND RANGE OF MIND

The mind of humankind is some part of the Mind of God, and therefore it contains within itself unlimited possibility for expansion and self-expression. The conscious mind of humankind is self-knowing. It knows and recognizes our true selves. It can range the entire universe to assemble knowledge of facts. It can take these facts, weigh them, balance them and arrive at conclusions. This ability to choose between evidences and to accept or reject them is the result of our conscious ability *to think independently of conditions.*

The Spirit is the only conscious intelligence in the universe. Because of this, it is the only directive intelligence in the universe. Our conscious mind, being part of the Mind of Spirit, is likewise directive. Thus we can mold the conditions in which we choose to live.

Since there is only one Mind in the universe, we know that it must be eternal. It is the first cause of all that is. But that Mind functions in different ways. In its self-knowing state, it is Spirit. In its automatic, impersonal, creative state, it is the law of Mind corresponding to the subjective mind of humankind.

This divine self-knowingness in us sets us apart from all creation. It is this which enables us to work out our own destiny according to a definite law of cause and effect, because our choosing and directive mind enables us to make our choices, and our accepting subjective mind enables us to carry out those choices on the environmental side of life. There is only one Mind, one law, one creation: the Mind, law and creation of God. God and we are one on all three levels of expression.

Everything Arises from Mind

In Universal Mind is contained everything that ever was, is or will be. Everything is there *in essence*. This is difficult for us to grasp, because our senses tell us that things originate in different ways or through different creative processes. Until we see clearly that Mind is the only creative agency in the universe, we are going to be puzzled by apparent incongruities in our study and practice. When we realize that all other *apparent* creative agencies are merely Mind working in different ways, we will see the singular unity running through every activity and every manifestation of power in the universe. When we grasp the truth that things exist in the Universal Mind as ideas and that ideas take form and become things as the result of the action of Mind within and upon itself, we are getting nearer to an understanding of the entire creative process.

The invisible essence of Mind is substance, which is unformed stuff or energy. This energy exists everywhere throughout the universe, waiting to take form. It takes form as we make our demand on ourselves. That is, Spirit in us is making its demand on Mind in us to give form to the essence of Mind. Universal Mind is making its demand on Mind in us to give form to the essence of Mind. Substance, while always ready to take form, is unable to do so because it lacks self-knowingness. Each of us, as Spirit, possesses self-knowingness. Therefore, when we make our demand, Mind brings its essence (substance) into form, and the creation or demonstration is made.

All of this may seem very abstract and far removed from the settlement of daily problems. On the contrary, it is the most practical and intimate knowledge possible and is fundamentally necessary to clear thinking. In the limitless surrounding ocean of Mind exists everything that we will ever demonstrate, even though it lies there in an unformed state. It can flow out into form *only under the directive word* of God and of you—God in the great world; you in the little world. Thus when you speak your word, the law of Mind responds just as it does to the directive word of God.

Mind in its unformed state, containing the potential of everything that we ever hope to accomplish or possess, can be called forth into individual use. All the resources of the universe are at our call. In our little world we get nothing except that which we have first formed as a mental concept or idea. Every dollar we ever make, every joy we ever experience, every surge of health we ever enjoy, the home we are to own, the business we are to build, all exist *now* in Mind, awaiting our mental formulation of them *within our own consciousness*. Every bit of business we ever do, every condition of health must come out of consciousness, because our mind is some part of that one creative Mind.

Both body and supply are plastic. *They are Mind held in form.* We should never lose sight of the reality of the plastic, spiritual nature of everything we ever touch. It is fluid in its origin and concrete in its manifestation. Without our recognition of its original plasticity, there can never be an intelligent calling of it into form. Ponder this deeply. It will repay you again and again.

The Giant Within

Our objective mind is limited. It receives those impressions that come through the senses. But our subjective mind is limitless because it is the Universal Mind individualized. Through this individualized subjective mind, we contact the law of the universe and thus make use of the Mind of God. It is a tremendous power that we are thus authorized to use, and this knowledge is staggering in its implications.

The law of Mind, being a law of reflection, responds to our use of it by making things correspond to thoughts. Thus we in our demonstration receive through the law exactly that which we are mentally able to embody. *Things are thoughts clothed in substance.* Through the law of correspondence, a tiny mental acceptance makes for a tiny demonstration. A large faith makes for a large demonstration. In other words, we hold up our mental concepts before the mirror of the law, which has no choice but to reflect them back to us, magnified, it is true, *but still our thought.* Of course, there is no large and small in reality.

This giant within and around us is helpless without specific direction. It has nothing to do and nowhere to go of itself. Unless it is directed, it will do nothing permanent for us. Our choice is its will, desire and purpose as far as Mind is concerned, and as we awaken to this fact, we then control the giant. We should use the law definitely, specifically and *with a conscious knowledge that we are using and directing it.* This is the reason that our conscious thought has power.

The Cornerstone of Treatment

We should seek to develop "feeling" in our treatments. Our mental acceptances should be filled with conviction, warmth and color. These are properties of the imagination and can be cultivated. The law responds to feeling more quickly than to any other mental attitude.

As we begin in this Science, we should first master the intellectual phases of the subject. We should get our facts straight. We must understand the principles underlying this philosophy and the various techniques involved. Our knowledge and understanding of the technical terms must be complete and thorough. But after we have mastered all of these factors, we should pass on to the higher ground of "feeling" and form intimacy with Spirit. There should come the deep inner conviction of the entire obedience, as well as nearness of the law. Then there comes that mystical experience of what might be called "the love of our desires and directions."

It is not enough to have a mere intellectual grasp of truth. There must be a blending of our person with these forces with which we work. This brings the feeling of reality into our work. Quite naturally, this "feeling" is the product of growth in the new life. Each demonstration makes it more vivid, because the "feeling" grows and intensifies as we become more and more convinced that law is responding to us and that we are co-workers with Spirit.

The person who spends fifteen minutes a day in contemplation of these things and the remainder of the time in careless thinking is not very likely to develop this valuable feeling quality that makes the difference between understanding the truth and making it work. There should be steady, systematic contemplation of the multiple sides of the one truth. It might be well for us to occupy our thoughts for a few days with the way the law performs its wonders within the human body, keeping our minds alive to the marvels of physical activity—the marvel of digestion, of elimination, of taste, of appetite, of the various cravings or hungers, or the intricate workings of the brain and nerves. When our attention is given to these things, it does not mean that we must concentrate our thought on them all the time, but it does mean that our mind will find an inner conviction of their intricacy growing within us and an accompanying faith in the intelligence behind them. This leads into the "feeling" we have been speaking about.

The marvels of the heavens could occupy our thoughts for weeks. The mystery of life as seen in plants, fruits and flowers, their germination, budding, growth and reproduction, their delicate coloring, their formation of honey or fruit, all of these things are beyond our power to duplicate. They are rich sources of the deep inner conviction that lend "feeling" to our treatment.

Insect life, as shown in a hive of bees or a colony of ants, is a fruitful field for the development of "feeling." Bird life, the parental instinct and the marvels of instinctive life in all kinds of animals, the wonders of chemistry, the atomic world, the voice of people and our ability to communicate thought by means of it, these and thousands of other sources are open to our minds. But we should be orderly in our meditation, taking time to surround our subjects with thoughtful contemplation.

It may be a matter of surprise to note the way in which thoughts enrich themselves as they are allowed to settle on a subject. A column in the newspaper, a word on the radio, a conversation in an office, an advertisement on a billboard may bring into one's consciousness the very thought that illumines the whole subject. While the mind is closed to knowledge, these things fall unheeded on our eyes or ears, but when we are "alive" to them, they jump out at us from the most unexpected places. Thus we become thinkers, a rarity that the world needs so much in these days.

Clear Thinking Versus Daydreaming

We should be very careful to distinguish between daydreaming and creative treatment. While the preceding suggestions are valuable in that they build up a body of thought on the various activities of the one Mind, they are not mental treatments. Mental treatment is a series of definite statements in Mind of something particular and specific that we wish Mind to create for us. The meditative activities are splendid for forming the background of our work, but the concrete results are produced by the exact activities known as *treatment*.

During treatment, we do not wish; we *know*. We do not dream; we state. We do not hope; we accept. We do not beg; we announce. We definitely select that which we wish, give it exactness, and declare it into manifestation knowing that our word will be acted on by the law. If we want five hundred dollars, we do not speak our word for "some money." We make it specific, and the mirror of the law before which we hold our concept reflects that exact thing back to us.

Not Forcing, But Letting

You should learn to think clearly and to allow the image of your thoughts to sink into the depths of the subjective state. You must always remember that force and the law are incompatible. We do not force our thoughts down; we relax and allow them to sink into this inner receptivity with confidence, power and conviction. Our individual subjective mind is our place in the universal creative law and immediately connects us with limitless power and energy.

We also distinguish between "holding thoughts" and holding things in thought. One is an attempt at an impossible coercion; the other is a mental acceptance. You must come back again and again to this point, because you will often find the tendency creeping in to force issues. You can tell when your attitude is incorrect by the sensation of strain. Always remember that there is no sense of strain in a good mental treatment. To hold thoughts through the exercise of willpower, as though you were pouring your mental power into the things, does no good because it uses only a tiny fraction of the power at your disposal. On the other hand, "to hold a thought" as though you were *letting* something happen is to use the greatest power of all. You "let go and let God."

If at any time you find yourself doubting your ability to use the law, you should let the problem go and come back to your own inner life, taking the necessary time to regain the consciousness that it is "not I, but the Creator within me that does the work." You must treat yourself until you do believe, because it is the inner mental acceptance that is the key to successful treating, not the sweat and toil of your individual mind.

Finally, remember that pure Spirit exists always at the center of all form. Of itself, it is always formless, but it is forever giving birth to form. The forms may come and go, but Spirit goes on forever. We have form, but we are some part of that core of Spirit. Since pure Spirit is at the center of everything and is always responding to our thought, there is no limit to its manifestation for us *except the limitations that we ourselves set.*

∾

Meditation

My mind is the region of action, centered in Infinite Mind, where all creation takes place. This Infinite Mind is God. God is the expresser of form, and as expressed form, there is no place where God is not apparent. Therefore, this expresser is in me, mine to acknowledge and receive. This expresser works for me by working through me, and my belief is the mold set for my acceptance. Every time I think, I open a channel for more expression. Every time I act on my thought, I use my belief in the Creative Expresser indwelling me. The more I increase my acceptance of infinite possibilities, the less discouraged I become. I dismiss all thought or belief in poverty, knowing there are no barriers in my way. God is my way, and I live in God now. I am not fearful of giving, because there is unlimited supply surrounding me. There is a law of increase. My part is to discover and distribute with intelligent understanding all the good I am entrusted with. I do not have to withhold any good. There is always enough for me to enjoy and to share with all who need what I can give.

∾

Questions

1. What is the distinction between Spirit and law?
2. Explain the idea that Mind is the only creative agency.
3. Explain the statement, "The invisible essence of Mind is substance."
4. What do we mean by "feeling" in treatment?
5. What do we mean by the expression "let go and let God"?

Answers

1. Spirit is self-conscious, self-knowing. Law is an impersonal and mechanical force.
2. All things exist in Mind as ideas. Ideas pass through the activity of law into form. This process of Spirit passing into form in consonance with the law of thought is creation.
3. Substance is Spirit and therefore invisible. In response to ideas, this substance passes into form, thus becoming visible.
4. By "feeling" in treatment we do not mean an emotional reaction, but an interior awareness of spiritual reality and a consequent recognition of the spiritual perfection of the person or condition we are treating.
5. By "let go and let God" we mean that we drop the sense of responsibility for the result of a treatment and leave it trustfully to the all-intelligent and all-powerful processes of Creative Mind.

The Use of Formulas

᠙

In spiritual mind healing, formulas have no meaning in themselves. One working in this field will soon discover that no two treatments are exactly alike. It is a certain state of consciousness that the practitioner seeks to embody in mental treatment. The words used are a spontaneous expression of this consciousness. "Out of the fullness of the heart, the mouth speaks." However, while no exact formula should be used, certain ways of thinking have proved most effective in the art and science of spiritual mind healing, because it is truly both an art and a science. It is a combination of technique and feeling, of conviction and intention, of willingness and faith, of expectation, enthusiasm and conscious direction.

Religious Beliefs

Generally speaking, it is wise in the first interview with someone coming to you for spiritual work to find out what your client's fundamental beliefs are, being careful never to destroy any spiritual foundation that your client may have, even though you feel that you could give them a better one. You must begin by building with the material at hand.

Nearly everyone has some spiritual conviction about life. We have never yet met anyone who didn't have some philosophy by which they lived, whether it was good or bad. It is well to find out what one's inner outlook on life is, to determine what one's fundamental affirmations and beliefs in life are, and to build on these. Never destroy anything until you are certain that you have something better to put in its place. You should equally be certain that that which you have will be acceptable. There is no use providing cornerstones that are not used.

Most people have some faith in God, and it is on this faith that you must build. Do not argue about this faith or try to change it. Build on it. Instead of using a lot of weighty arguments to substantiate your point, let your clients do this for you. Let them explain to you what they believe and why, and actually help them to build this belief into something better. For instance, if a client says, "I do not understand metaphysics or the Science of Mind, but I do believe in prayer," say to this person, "That is all that is necessary. This is merely our way of praying."

Be sure that you permit your clients to pray in their own way, or else you will destroy without building up. You will take away without adding to. Be certain to avoid any confusion. Tell your clients that your prayer has been the most effective thing in the world and that you have nothing to add to their faith or conviction about God which is sacred to them alone. You do not commune for them, but with them. You are not trying to convert them. This will at once relieve both strain and antagonism.

How to Begin

A quiet, calm talk is a good starting point for a prayer session. Let your clients tell you exactly how they feel and why they feel as they do. Let them uncover their secret fears and faiths, but do not mentally crowd them in doing this. Lead rather than drive. It takes patience, calmness, poise and a great belief in the fundamental goodness of humanity. Love and understanding are the keynotes of this practice. Practitioners should never sit in judgment on their clients. Remember that both mistake (sin) and consequence (punishment) are only two ends of the same negative sequence of cause and effect. Never assume a "holier than thou" attitude or a "look at me and die" feeling. Get what the psychologist calls the "we" feeling. This should not be assumed; it should be sincere. It must be sincere, or else your clients will feel its insincerity.

Always begin your work by silently declaring that there is no fear and nothing of which to be afraid. Remove any sense of condemnation, judgment or punishment. Work to remove the sense of bondage and restriction. Always proceed on the assumption that there is something wonderful about your clients, something triumphant and transcendent, something God-like. Point this out to them in your conversation and realize it in your treatment.

Encourage Your Clients

Praise rather than blame. Encourage your clients to believe in themselves, pointing out that the real self is some part of God. This self is always strong and reliant. Make your clients feel mentally comfortable in your presence. Don't be afraid to unbend a little and be human. Smile a little, be natural and become interested in them and in what they are doing. Let them unburden their minds, and when they have done this, ask them to become quiet for a few moments while you treat them. If they ask you what treatment is, explain to them that you are endeavoring to realize that they are a perfect spiritual being, that they have a perfect relationship with the Supreme Power. Tell them that you are merely joining with them in declaring the truth about their real nature. Inwardly, however, you must know the truth about them, because when it comes to the silent treatment, you are transposing thoughts of unhappiness into those of joy. You are using the divine alchemy of Spirit with which to transform inaction into action, pain into peace, confusion into harmony.

Above all, learn to trust yourself. Learn to believe in your own method. Learn to have confidence in what you are doing, because this is all important. If clients come to you who suffer from asthma, for example, have a definite conviction that your word will relive every sense of tension or bondage or restriction. Treat until you have such a complete inner feeling of freedom for them that the contemplation of their suffering from asthma is no longer possible for you.

If you are treating those who have a sense of loneliness, not only explain to them that they are one with God and therefore with all people and all events, but work silently until this consciousness of unity dawns within your own thought, not merely as an intellectual statement, but as a deep inward feeling. This conviction will demonstrate friendship. Treat everyone who comes to you for a conviction that they belong to the universe, that they are worthwhile. There is no successful or permanent healing without a restoration of confidence and faith—faith in the self, faith in God, faith in destiny.

In your audible talks with your clients, explain that the spiritual nature that they already have is the real foundation of their life. You are not trying to give them faith; you are merely trying to redirect the faith that they already have. This is most important, and good results inevitably follow when this procedure is carried out. Teach your clients to mentally identify themselves with success, with happiness and with friendship. Explain to them that if they do this, the doorway of opportunity will open before them. Then, when you treat them silently, know that the door already is open. *You must also know that they enter that doorway.* You must work, then, not only to know that they exist at the point of supply, which is always available to them, but you must know that they avail themselves of this supply. There is not only an intelligence within them that knows what they ought to do, but this same intelligence compels them to do what should be done.

Be Specific

Abstract statements are useless unless they are followed by those that connect such statements with the people for whom you are working. For instance, it is not enough to say, "God is your friend." You must follow this statement by saying that since there is one Mind in which all people live, and since this Mind is friendly, then those for whom you are working are friends to everyone whom they meet. And since they are friends to everyone they meet, then everyone they meet will respond to them in a friendly manner. What you heal is the thought of loneliness, separation, division and disunity by substituting a consciousness of oneness that includes all the people your clients will ever meet. God is not only everywhere, but God is personified to your clients through everyone whom they meet. It is not enough merely to state that good *is*; the good that *is* is your client's good. Do not forget that your word is the enforcement of this divine law of goodness. This goodness is pushed into personal experience and becomes your clients' goodness.

Practitioners must not only state that evil has no power, but we must *know* that it has none, otherwise our statements will have no effect. In a certain sense, you gather your clients into your own consciousness and surround them with a realization of life, and for each realization you make, you state that this is the law in their experience and that this law is manifesting in their person and in their affairs at this moment.

In spiritual treatment, we should realize the Divine Presence as being perfect and complete within itself and then follow this by realizing that our clients are in this Divine Presence and this Divine Presence is in them. The two are really one: one in purpose, one in power and one in execution. Therefore, if any of your clients say, "I lack the judgment to know how to get along in life," try to realize for them that there is only one Mind, one intelligence. This Mind and this intelligence, being the only Mind there is, is also the Mind of your clients. This Mind is governing, directing and controlling them. It compels them to make right decisions. Think of this Mind as being at the very center of their being, not as something that descends into them or as something that operates from a center already established.

This is a good way to proceed in working for business improvement. Generally in such instances you should work to know that there is no inaction, but that right action is always taking place in the experience of your clients. They always know what to do and how to do it, because the Divine is always at the center of their being. First, we convince ourselves that this is the truth about our clients.

The Consciousness of the Practitioner

The result of a mental treatment cannot reach a level higher than the level of consciousness from which the treatment is given. This is self-evident, because we are dealing with a law of cause and effect. Hence, if you appear to fail, start right over again—begin at the beginning. Forget that you have failed. Forget that you have ever treated this particular person before. Start over in a new way, approaching a solution of the problem with a fresh spontaneity, a new outlook. If your treatment seems repetitious and monotonous, stop for awhile and begin to think of something else, and then return to the treatment with a new vision.

You will soon discover that all practitioners work out their own methods, but of course all methods must conform to the principle if they are to be effective. Having conformed to the principle, do not be afraid to take considerable leeway in its application, otherwise your work will fail to be spontaneous and will be ineffective. Never forget that your treatments are given in your own mind for your clients. After you have talked the situation over with them and they have told you why they are suffering from negative conditions, be those in body or the body of their affairs, and after you have listened to all these reasons why the good that they desire has not been or cannot be, after you have finished your audible conversation with them and have begun your silent work for them, you must in your thought cover the negation that they have revealed in their conversation with you. You are building up a realization about them that is exactly opposite to the one that they had for themselves.

In this silent treatment, you pay no attention to the case history, as though it were a condition of itself. You may use denials. You may use affirmations and realization. You may repeat thoughts that come to you or that you have heard and believed in. Mentally you may pray, sing, dance or exult. Follow your own lead at any particular instance, but always be certain that there is a definite intention running through your treatment. This intention is that you clients will be relieved of everything that is wrong, and in its place everything that is right will enter and become a part of their experience, mentally, physically and spiritually. You must not only believe this, but you must know that what you believe about them is really true. You must also know that they realize this.

Now here is a very subtle thought. When I say that you must know that they realize this, I do not mean that you are trying mentally to convince them of anything. *You are trying to convince yourself.* In no sense is this to be confused with any form of mental coercion. It is merely an important point in your inner realization for your clients. The Spirit within you is bearing witness to the Spirit within them, that there is one Spirit in which you both believe, one good that is always available, one life that forever flows. It is your business to know that this life takes the form of perfection in your clients, for them and through them.

Follow your own hunch, but be sure that your hunch is in line with principle. Loosen the reins of your spiritual imagination, believing that everything you say and think is true in the experience of your clients. It is impossible to fail in producing good results if you follow this method.

Repeating Treatments

How often should you repeat a treatment? You should continue treating until the desired results are obtained. Of course, this does not mean continuous treatment. Once a day perhaps, possible two or three times a day when necessary, but never carrying the client around in your thought. Each treatment should be complete within itself and then left alone. Forget it, but if necessary pick it up again at a later time. Never try to repeat the treatment exactly as you gave it before, but always seek to embody the main points using new ideas and approaches on each occasion.

The power to heal and to help is in every person because the principle of life is in all. It is a power that everyone possesses but few have consciously used. You are learning to use this power consciously for yourself and others. Live in the belief that everyone who contacts you will be benefited. Believe that everyone who thinks of you will receive an uplift. Live in the expectation that every constructive word you speak will have an instantaneous, a perfect and a permanent result. Know that nothing but good can go from you and nothing but good can return to you. Practitioners should treat themselves daily to know that their work is both perfect, permanent and instantaneous in its manifestation.

Each victory will help you to win another. A practitioner's work should be cumulative. There is no such thing as losing spiritual power, because power is eternal in the universe and forever available. No one ever gets away from God or outside of Spirit. No one ever divorces themselves from life. It is the business of practitioners in this Science to be so filled with the realization of life that it automatically imparts itself to everyone whom they contact. In this way, your light will shine in the darkness of human experience. It will become a beacon sending its rays across the storm-tossed lives of those in distress.

What Makes Good Practitioners?

Who are good practitioners? First, they are those who know that life *is* and is perfect. Next, they are those who know that what they know is power. Hence, there are no good practitioners unless such practitioners first know that they are good practitioners. We should realize that there is only one healer; this is the Spirit of truth. There is only one life principle; this is God in us. There is only one final law; this is the law of good. There is only one ultimate impulsion; this impulsion is love. As we array this concept of God against the false evidence of all appearances, we must be certain that the conclusions we draw from our arguments and processes of reasoning and intuitive perceptions outweigh all evidence that would contradict them. The winning or losing of a demonstration lies entirely in your state of consciousness, in whether or not you really are able to perceive more good than not, to have your consciousness of joy transcend your acceptance of grief.

A practitioner must have a calm that transcends the distorted thought and confusion of the client. We must have a sense of eternal justice that outweighs any belief in or manifestation of temporary injustice. We must have a sense of a law of abundance that completely transmutes the lesser concept from bondage into liberty. It is not enough for us merely to know this or to state it as our belief or to affirm it as a conviction. This is only the foundation on which we build our edifice of faith. These are the materials that we hold into the form of definite desire. We must not only know that God is all there is, but we must know that God exists right where the need is. Being all-in-all, God has no opposition, competition or otherness.

⌒⌒

Meditation

I am surrounded by an Infinite Mind, an all-knowing intelligence that receives my attitudes of Mind and tends to reflect them into experiences. I am indwelt by a conscious living Spirit that is the center and source of my being. I recognize my unity with this self-directive, self-knowing Spirit and my ability to use the creative law of Mind. Today I consciously direct this law to bring me an abundance of love, of friendship, of health and of supply. I know that these things now come to me because the invincible law is acting in accordance with my desire. It is done unto me according to my faith.

⌒

Questions

1. Should we argue with our clients about their religious convictions?
2. Is mental coercion used in this Science?
3. How long should one continue to treat a client?
4. Who has the power to heal?
5. Is it possible to lose the power?

Answers

1. We should never argue with our clients about their religious convictions. We must be careful not to destroy anything until there is something better and more acceptable to put in its place.
2. Mental coercion is never attempted in the Science of Mind. The reason for this is that practitioners work in their own minds for the clients.
3. Treat until the thing you are working for takes place.
4. Everyone has the power to heal, because all have access to the one Mind and the one power.
5. It is impossible to lose the power to help or heal. The power *is*, and we use it. It is always and eternally available.

Life Is What You Make It

In the first chapter, we stated that "Life is what you make it." Of course, we did not mean that anything we as individuals do can change the nature of reality; it is self-evident that we cannot do this. What we can do is to change our individual relationship to reality so that it presents us with new and happier experiences. This is the mission of the Science of Mind and Spirit.

If we wish to "make life our servant instead of our master," we must come to understand what the laws of nature are and comply with them. Since this is true of physical laws, it must equally be true of mental and spiritual laws, and in these chapters we have come to understand that the laws of Mind and Spirit are as definite as other laws of nature with which we are acquainted.

We have established a principle of Mind, just as in another science it has been established that there is a principle of electricity. We have concluded that this Mind principle is the final absolute and only creative power in the universe. In doing this, we have not departed from what would be considered scientific procedure in any field of knowledge. Just as it has been established that there is only one ultimate electric energy, so we have assumed that there is only one ultimate Mind. Just as electric energy operating through a bulb will light a particular space without in any way departing from its original nature, so we have assumed that, in like manner, the mentality of each individual is some part of the Universal Mind. To state it another way, there is one Universal Mind that each person individualizes to a greater or lesser degree.

It is this simple but fundamental fact in our philosophy that differentiates its mental practice from the field of willpower, suggestion, mental concentration and endeavor to coerce or from any control to force anything. We have also established the idea that the universe consists of pure Spirit, which is infinite knowingness, absolute law, the potentiality of infinite doingness and limitless substance that forever takes the form of creation. We have assumed what the inspired of all ages have proclaimed: that the divine reality itself never changes, although it is forever taking temporary form. This assumption is backed by every scientific discovery that has yet been made, and as far as we know it has never had any logical argument or known fact to contradict it. Energy is indestructible, and whatever that substance is which is forever taking form, nothing is either added to or taken from it. Therefore, we have concluded that all change is a play of life upon itself. It is this inner movement of the creative principle upon itself which constitutes its sole and only activity.

With the inspired of the ages, we have concluded that the universe consists of pure Spirit that has an irresistible urge toward self-expression, backed by an absolute law of cause and effect, which is the servant of the eternal Spirit throughout the ages. Humankind's place in this creative order is to reproduce, on the scale of the individual life, the same creative function that the Spirit exercises in the life of the cosmos.

At first, we are ignorant of our true nature. Consequently, because of our limited vision, we have bound ourselves by the very law (cause and effect) by which we might as easily have produced freedom. We have created an apparent duality out of an absolute unity, and we have suffered the consequences. As ignorance has been our besetting sin or mistake, so enlightenment must become our salvation through the knowledge of our true relationship to the cosmos.

Throughout the ages, there have been those who by intuition have arrived at these conclusions and by faith have demonstrated the transcendent nature of reality as it flows through the consciousness of humankind. We have sought to discover the secret of their power, and we feel that we have established this secret as being nothing more mysterious than a firm conviction that the Invisible responds to us and measures out its creativeness to us through our thought, will, imagination and inner conviction. We have also arrived at the conclusion—which we feel is self-evident—that divine creativeness is delivered to us only in such degree as we ourselves recognize that we share the creative power. This seems self-evident, because the universe cannot be divided against itself. Therefore, we are justified in believing that our use of this creative power must always be in exact proportion to the recognition of our own unity with good.

From the creative power of thought, which we all possess, there is no escape. It merely becomes a question of how we will use it. To state the proposition in the simplest manner, there is an infinite thinker forever thinking itself into form. There is an infinite law forever acting on its thought, and creation is the result. We are each some part of this process. Our thought is creative not because we will it to be so, but because that is its nature.

Since the Infinite Creative can never be in opposition to itself (because it would then be self-destructive), its fundamental nature is beneficence, goodness, truth and beauty. Only in such degree as the individual life imbibes this nature does it have real power. It is also true that any destructive use of the law of cause and effect has the power of ultimately destroying its own embodiment. We feel that history proves that this principle is correct.

If the foregoing conclusions are correct, it follows that wherever any individual or group of individuals reverses the use of the law and complies with its harmony, such a person or group must automatically prosper. This brings us to a practical application of this principle, because it is to its correct use that the world must look for the salvation that it so greatly needs, both individually and collectively.

There is an irresistible urge within us to be happy, to be whole and to express life in a less limited way. This urge is cosmic and therefore divine. This latent divinity stirs within our imagination and, due to its insistent demand, impels and compels our evolution. It is behind every invention. It proclaims itself through all prophetic utterances. It has produced sages, saints and saviors, and will when permitted create a new world order from which war, pestilence and famine will have vanished.

You and I cannot instantly change the thought of the world. It is self-evident that we must begin at the only center from which we could operate, and that is ourselves. There is nothing selfish about this, because as an ever-growing group of individuals comes to understand and apply these principles, just so surely will this new world order be born into human experience. We must begin to reconstruct the individual life. It is for this purpose that we study the Science of Mind and Spirit. We desire to capture and make use of the subtle power that the inspired of the ages have proclaimed to be available to every individual.

The most simple and direct approach that anyone can make to this divine reality is one of childlike acceptance. That is why the realm of God has been likened to a child. Those wishing to demonstrate the supremacy of spiritual thought force, whether it be in physical healing or in bringing about the betterment of circumstances for themselves and others, must become intellectually and spiritually convinced that in such degree as their thought is in line with reality, it is no longer separated from power, but itself *is* power. How could it be otherwise if there is only one ultimate Mind that we all use?

It is not enough merely to become convinced of spiritual power or that we have access to power, because this is merely a statement of our conviction and affirmation of our belief. There is a vast difference between announcing a spiritual philosophy and making definite use of a universal principle. We must not only understand this spiritual philosophy, we must *consciously apply it* to the problems of everyday life. Theory without practice will never accomplish anything worthwhile. Science of Mind, with its definite technique for mental practice, is a statement of principles coupled with a method for procedure. It not only affirms that God, the universal Spirit, is supreme; it follows this affirmation with the declaration. Because this creative principle is active in human affairs, it is doing something for us right now. It is passing through our will, translating our feeling, imagination and conviction into activity.

The practical application of this principle is a thing of thought, and its technique is a certain way of thinking. And here is the crux of the whole matter. Practitioners in this field feel that we are using power that is independent of any existing circumstance, because it can make a new condition as easily as it can perpetuate the old. But as far as we are concerned, it can create the new condition only in accordance with the pattern of our thought. Because we are individuals, we must initiate the new pattern ourselves. In this way, we are co-workers, co-creators with the Infinite.

There is no possible danger that can come from the use of this power, because it is delivered to us only in such degree as we partake of its Spirit, which must be harmony, unity and love. It is good to remind ourselves that the universe is foolproof and that the secret place of the Most High is never violated. It is impossible to use real spiritual power for any purpose that is destructive, and the wise person will never make this futile attempt.

Assuming, then, that we desire to identify ourselves with this Spirit of reality, for what purposes may we legitimately feel that this power can be used? The answer seems self-evident. We may use it for any purpose that increases livingness, joy, constructive self-expression, happiness, peace and wholeness. Just as light overcomes darkness merely because it is light, so a realization of our unity with good erases negative experience.

It is a basic principle in our Science that the idea of good will always destroy the idea of evil, whereas the idea of evil has no power over good. Good remains supreme, inviolate.

The tools that practitioners in this field use are thoughts. These thoughts have a power equal to our conviction and will always manifest themselves at the level of our consciousness, whether we are speaking our word for ourselves or for someone else. Our whole philosophy assumes that we are living in a spiritual universe governed by laws of thought; that thoughts of destruction will finally destroy their own embodiment and consume themselves, while constructive thought must, because of its nature, heal any condition that comes under its beneficent influence.

One must feel that there is no finality to evil other than oblivion, while the finality of good is always certain. Let us again remind ourselves that no one has ever seen a principle in nature, and yet we are always demonstrating that such principles really exist. Those who deny that right thought, consciously directed, has power are those who are entirely ignorant both of this principle and of its practice. The only person who can speak with any authority is the one who has accepted the principle and who has put it to the test of actual practice. Such a one will never deny its potency.

Therefore, be not at all concerned over anything other than your own attitude toward the truth, because there is a truth that, once known, becomes demonstrated. There is a freedom that in a degree we may prove to be active in our own experience. It would have been a complete waste of your valuable time to have studied these principles and then failed to make conscious use of them. Since the only place you can start is within yourself, begin at once to use the power that is already within you. Do not wait for a greater understanding, because the use of a law is the only thing that broadens one's knowledge of it.

The laws of Mind are no different from other laws of nature; they exist but must be used. Feel that your word is the enforcement of this law and that wherever, whenever and for whatsoever or whomsoever you speak your word, the living, creative power swings into action, ready, willing and able to create and to recreate. Never confuse this with willpower. Never feel that you must hold thoughts or concentrate either mind or mental attention on anything. Spiritual treatment is an active mental presentation to your own thought of your inner conviction. This mental presentation must be so formed as to have definite action in the direction that you give it.

When you give a mental treatment, you have a definite intention in your mind. Your treatment is given for a specific purpose. Let us assume that it is for someone's physical healing. You become quiet within your own thought, reassure yourself of the reality of the power with which you are dealing, erect an altar of faith in the sanctuary of your own consciousness, and then declare that your word is for the person you are treating. This directs your treatment for that person rather than for someone else. All treatment should have conscious direction and definite intention. Next you make a series of statements that should automatically flow out of your conviction. There is no magic in words. The statements used are not deliberately thought out; they flow spontaneously from your consciousness. However, these statements should always cover the need.

If you are treating others for increased activity in their affairs, your statement must be so formulated as to convey the idea of activity to your own consciousness. What you really are doing is creating an idea of activity for these people. You are not trying to mentally convince anyone of anything; you are mentally convincing yourself about them. Therefore, you are freed from any burden of thought as to whether or not they are receiving the treatment. Your whole endeavor is to convince yourself about those for whom you are treating, to assure yourself that there is a divine activity in their affairs, that this activity is functioning in everything they do; it is surrounding them with love and friendship; it goes before them and prepares their way; it opens the doorway of opportunity to them; it compels them to make right judgments, to act intelligently; it inspires both their thought and their acts. Everything that they do prospers. You might also state, if it seems necessary, that your word removes doubt, fear, uncertainty, and glorifies the consciousness. The Spirit enlightens your client's mind and gives enthusiastic buoyancy to your client's acts.

Experience will gradually teach you just what statements are necessary in individual cases. Speaking from the general theory of practice, your treatment should cover whatever seems necessary in each individual case. For instance, if those for whom you are treating should say to you that they cannot succeed because they lack the opportunity to reveal any qualifications they may have, it would be your business as a practitioner to state that the opportunity does present itself; that they are free to express every quality that they possess. If those for whom you are helping should tell you that there is too much competition in their field, your declaration about them would be so stated as to cover the thought of competition. You might declare that since they represent the perfected Spirit and the complete unity of good, there is no competition. You would not be trying to destroy competition, but rather to eradicate the belief in competition. As far as your clients are concerned, this is all that would be necessary. This is what we would mean by saying that, in treatment, we must cover whatever seems necessary. Experience alone can teach us to do this, but one will never gain the experience unless one begins to use the principle.

❧

We are reluctant to bring this series of chapters to a close, not because we are fearful, but because we are so desirous of emphasizing the few simple facts that are fundamental to the practice of this Science. Our whole desire is to impart to you a knowledge that will give you conscious use of the power that you already possess, to place in your hands the tools with which to use this principle, and to be certain that our explanation has been sufficiently clear so that no doubt as to your ability to make conscious use of the Science of Mind can remain in your thought.

The supreme test in this, as in other things, is in the use you make of it.

Remember that the biggest life is the one that includes the most. We are all part of some cosmic wholeness. The more good we set in motion, the more of that good must come back to us. As Walt Whitman said, "The gift is most to the giver and comes back the most to the giver."

ERNEST SHURTLEFF HOLMES (1887–1960), an ordained Divine Science minister, was founder of a spiritual movement known as Religious Science, a part of the New Thought movement, whose spiritual philosophy is known as Science of Mind. He was the author of *The Science of Mind* and numerous other metaphysical books, as well as founder of *Science of Mind* magazine, in continuous publication since 1927.

NEWT LIST is the foremost publisher of updated editions of spiritual classic texts. Newt List titles are edited to provide contemporary language structure and idioms that have evolved since the original manuscript was published. We revise punctuation and capitalizations, and adjust sentence structure when appropriate, as well as update certain words or terms that have since become obscure, as long as those changes do not affect the author's intention or meaning. More valuable for readers today, though, is Newt List's procedure of changing of gender forms. In the time of original publication, these classic books generally used masculine forms when referring to God or humankind. Newt List updates all its books using gender-neutral language, making the ideas in them apply more broadly to all readers.

Newt List Editor Randall Friesen brings years of experience editing and publishing spiritual texts. For many years, Randall worked at Science of Mind Publishing, editing and publishing the words and ideas of Ernest Holmes and other authors of spirituality in the role of Publisher of its book division and Editor-in-Chief of *Science of Mind* magazine. For Newt List, Randall has edited these valuable manuscripts to retain the author's voice while at the same time enhancing the originality and vitality of the ideas for today, making them accessible to more people.

NewtList.com

Made in the USA
Thornton, CO
12/15/24 19:43:06